COLOSSIANS

Another Commentary
on an
Inexhaustible Message

Gordon H. Clark

The Trinity Foundation
Jefferson, Maryland

Copyright 1979,
Lois A. Zeller and
Elizabeth Clark George.
Second Edition ©
1989, The Trinity Foundation
Post Office Box 169
Jefferson, Maryland 21755

ISBN 0-940931-25-7

Contents

Foreword 5

Preface 7

The First Chapter 13

The Second Chapter 69

The Third Chapter 109

The Fourth Chapter 125

Appendix 133

Index 137

Scripture Index 147

The Crisis of Our Time 151

Intellectual Ammunition 159

Books by Gordon H. Clark

Readings in Ethics (1931)
Selections from Hellenistic Philosophy (1940)
A History of Philosophy (coauthor, 1941)
A Christian Philosophy of Education (1946, 1988)
A Christian View of Men and Things (1952)
What Presbyterians Believe (1956)[1]
Thales to Dewey (1957)
Dewey (1960)
Religion, Reason and Revelation (1961, 1986)
William James (1963)
Karl Barth's Theological Method (1963)
The Philosophy of Science and Belief in God (1964, 1987)
What Do Presbyterians Believe? (1965, 1985)
Peter Speaks Today (1967)[2]
The Philosophy of Gordon H. Clark (1968)
Biblical Predestination (1969)[3]
Historiography: Secular and Religious (1971)
II Peter (1972)[2]
The Johannine Logos (1972)
Three Types of Religious Philosophy (1973, 1989)
First Corinthians (1975)
Colossians (1979, 1989)
Predestination in the Old Testament (1979)[3]
I and II Peter (1980)
Language and Theology (1980)
First John (1980)
God's Hammer: The Bible and Its Critics (1982, 1987)
Behaviorism and Christianity (1982)
Faith and Saving Faith (1983)
In Defense of Theology (1984)
The Pastoral Epistles (1984)
The Biblical Doctrine of Man (1984)
The Trinity (1985)
Logic (1985, 1988)
Ephesians (1985)
Clark Speaks From the Grave (1986)
Logical Criticisms of Textual Criticism (1986)
First and Second Thessalonians (1986)
Predestination (1987)
The Atonement (1987)
The Incarnation (1988)

[1] Revised in 1965 as *What Do Presbyterians Believe?*
[2] Combined in 1980 as *I & II Peter.*
[3] Combined in 1987 as *Predestination.*

Foreword

When Paul wrote his letter to the Colossians, he was a prisoner of Caesar, perhaps at Rome. Rome was a major city, the center of the Empire; Colosse was a small and declining town in what we now call Turkey, more than a thousand miles from Rome. At one time Colosse had been a great city; by the eighth century it was abandoned; today its site is still uninhabited.

Despite Paul's distance from Colosse, despite his never having been at Colosse, and despite his status as a prisoner—or perhaps because of all these reasons and more—Paul wrote a short letter of about two thousand words to correct an error growing in the church at Colosse. In that letter he emphasized the all-sufficiency of Jesus Christ as creator, redeemer, mediator, and source of knowledge.

Paul's message is one that needs as much emphasis today as it did in the first century. The various empty deceits of the twentieth century include attacks on both the deity and humanity of Christ, on the doctrine of creation, on the need for and the possibility of redemption, on Christ as the sole mediator between God and men, and on Christ's Word as the sole source of truth. Paul, good minister of Christ that he was, and despite his status as a prisoner of Rome, instructed the first century Christians in the faith, and so instructs us as well.

Many professing American Christians, like some professing

5

Foreword

Colossian Christians, believe and teach the insufficiency of Christ, either in salvation proper, or in philosophy. Paul specifically criticized the worldly philosophy that was seducing the Colossians, and he emphasized that because *all* the treasures of wisdom and knowledge are in Christ, we are to beware lest anyone cheat us through empty and deceptive philosophy based on the traditions of men, on the basic principles of the world, and not on Christ's Word.

Ever since the first century, many who consider themselves both wise and Christians have embraced worldly philosophy and so have cheated themselves and others. They have not understood or not believed Paul's message: the all-sufficiency of Christ. For this reason, and with a prayer that God will grant the reader both understanding and assent, we are pleased to republish this commentary on Paul's extraordinary letter to the Colossians. May it help twentieth century Christians understand and believe the all-sufficiency of Christ in both theology and philosophy.

John W. Robbins
November 25, 1988

Preface

On my desk lie several commentaries on Colossians. One has 112 pages. It is not very good. Another, by a French Huguenot, has 685 pages! It is somewhat better. The aim of the present commentary is to clarify and explain Paul's message to the Colossians. This cannot be well done in 112 pages; but something of value hardly needs 685. Here many extraneous matters have been deliberately excluded. No time is spent on Greek civilizations, nor on the geography, history, economics, or culture of Colosse—except insofar as the epistle itself discloses the religious condition of the church members there. Not even the question of authorship, a regular topic in so-called introductions to the New Testament, is debated. The liberals lost that battle a long time ago. Now they can hardly make a plausible case against II Peter. Accordingly, this commentary studies only the message.

With respect to the religious situation in the Colossian church, it may be wise to include in this preface certain remarks on Gnosticism. Some commentators believe that this religious system, which actually menaced the very existence of Christianity in the second century, was influential in first-century Colosse, and that Paul in this letter considered it a major matter of concern. Lightfoot takes this view, and time after time in his commentary states that Paul in this verse had Gnosticism in view. However, one should not too quickly make such an assumption. Liberal scholars have sometimes tried to make Christianity its offshoot. Reitzenstein argued that Paul derived his theory of redemption from pre-Christian Gnosticism, or at least the Hermetic literature and the mysteries. Two difficulties attach to Reitzenstein's view. First, although Hermes, the Gnostics, and Paul spoke about redemption, their theories on the nature and method of redemption are so different that neither could have been derived from the other. It is true that the Gnostics spoke about Jehovah and Christ; but Jehovah was a second-rate somewhat ignorant god, and there were several Christs of varying compositions. Second, there is no good evidence of any pre-Christian Gnosticism at all.

Simon Magus may have been the originator of a very early form of Gnosticism. Basilides and Valentinus, who gave it its standard form, came a century later. Even *Poimander*, the first tractate of Hermes Trismegistus, is usually dated at A.D. 125; and yet Poimander has a better claim to be older Egyptian religion than any Gnosticism has. It is barely possible that some simple incipient Gnostic ideas were emerging in Colosse, but it is doubtful that Paul was addressing himself particularly to that form of religion. His message is more general.

Lightfoot tries to take care of these objections by positing a combination of Essene asceticism and Gnosticism in first-century Colosse. Strangely (p. 106) he identifies Cerinthus as "the intermediate link" between the two religions. Maybe so, but Cerinthus came near the end of the century and could not have influenced the Colossians during Paul's lifetime. And Lightfoot admits (p. 108) "Nor is there [in the Colossian epistle] any trace of later Gnosticism." What this amounts to is a redefinition of Gnosticism. Instead of using the thirty eons as the definitive characteristic of Gnosticism, Lightfoot extends the term to cover a variety of religious themes.

Herbert M. Carson (*Colossians and Philemon*, Eerdmans, 1960, pp. 16–17) has similar doubts about the Gnostics, but suggests that Paul is opposing a Greek view of the antagonism between matter and spirit, for the object of Paul's denunciations is not licentiousness, as in other epistles, but asceticism. This asceticism led to a false humility expressed in the worship of angel-mediators. However, Carson acknowledges that we do not know how far such ideas had developed.

Lightfoot's suggestion of Essene influence to account for asceticism is better than Carson's Greek thesis—even though it is hard to show that there were any Essenes in Colosse. At any rate, asceticism was not a popular Greek view. Even Plato, whose phrase "the body is a tomb" is so well known, was no ascetic. The Greek philosophers were not extremists, unless it be the Cynics and Cyrenaics, whose schools hardly survived the death of Aristotle. Aside from the philosophers, who were no more popular than they are today—see Aristophanes' *Clouds*—the Greek populace chiefly admired the superb bodies of their great athletes. The Olympics, not the Lyceum, not the Stoa, made all the headlines. And as in Paul's Corinth, the Greek vice was licentiousness. This was not true of the Colossian church, though what the small town of Colosse and the still smaller church were like in detail we can hardly say. Paul concerns himself with the church's shortcomings, but it is risky to tie them in with any widespread philosophical or religious movement.

In contrast with these views on the origin of the false doctrines, Nigel Turner (*Grammatical Insights into the New Testament*, p. 122) supposes that "a humanist philosophy had become fashionable at Colosse. . . . It was based on physical science and was materialistic." Turner gives no evidence whatever to support this supposition. On the face of it, it is unlikely because Colosse does not seem to have been the intellectual center of the age, and because "the philosophy of our own age of Enlightenment" is quite out of harmony with the most widely spread forms of Greek culture. Even Turner acknowledges that their age superstitiously engaged in astrology and the black arts. Is this the "Enlightenment"?

It seems best therefore to be most cautious in identifying the heathen views in Colosse. Whatever the origin of the pagan ideas Paul is combatting, those ideas are more like Gnosticism than humanism. But one must hew close to the Pauline text. Paul's message is of a very general character, fortunately indeed, because such generality makes it applicable to present day conditions in a way that Gnostic themes could never be. In America, and in the world for that matter, there are two contrasting, antagonistic viewpoints, both of which have some considerable following. The more numerous, and in widespread opinion the more respectable, group embraces naturalistic, behavioristic, humanistic secularism. These people are not all technical philosophers or scientists. Most of them pick up their opinions from the public schools and state universities, as well as from popular periodicals. They may have heard of Freud; they probably do not know Ryle and Skinner. Therefore they express themselves in ordinary English—as a girl in one of my university classes remonstrated with me by asserting, "Well, I am only an animal." Incidentally this is an opinion no animal would have asserted.

These people do not believe in God, nor in angels, nor in a life after death; and discussion of heaven or of an intermediate state are all nonsense to them. In antiquity also there were such people; but unlike the present century they were then a minority.

The second group is very religious. In antiquity they were a majority, as Acts 17:22 attests. They believed in many gods, including demons and spirits of various kinds; they believed in a future life, and practiced the rites of several religions. The Gnostics formed a subdivision of this extremely large group. Today there is a recrudescence of similar views. Such people take seriously the astrology column in the newspapers; they consult mediums to contact the dead; and some worship the devil. Paul speaks to both groups. Against the former he asserts the reality of spiritual beings; against the latter he describes a spiritual world quite different from theirs.

For this reason it is useful to have a clear understanding of what precisely Paul meant. And the aim of this commentary is to help the reader achieve such understanding.

There are difficulties. First, there is the difficulty of translating Greek into English. Here the reader who knows no Greek must accede to the translator's assertion that the Greek word *Logos* means *word* (or, mathematical ratio, sentence, book, description, doctrine, and not less than a score of other words that in one way or another designate some expression of reason). So far as vocabulary is concerned, the student without Greek has to depend on his professor. This should not discourage him. Of course a knowledge of Greek is useful. To the scholar it is indispensable. Automotive engineering is also indispensable to technicians, but the rest of us drive in blissful ignorance. With respect to the New Testament the really important difficulties do not concern the meanings of individual Greek words. No competent scholar of professional reputation will wittingly deceive his readers on matters of simple vocabulary. He should and usually does inform the reader of the several possible meanings of a word. The difficulty comes in construing the sentence or the paragraph. Given the possible meanings and presented with alternate interpretations, he who knows no Greek can yet make tolerably good judgments as to which interpretation is preferable.

Then, too, difficulties come in different sizes. Some are trivial or easy; others substantial and perplexing. The first few pages of this commentary may seem to wander from the text because the text of the salutation requires so little explanation. If the paragraph on textual criticism gives the impression of pedantic triviality, and thus irritates the reader, he might pause to consider two or three things. First, the general question of textual criticism is of more importance in personal assurance, evangelistic endeavor, and certainly in doctrinal study, than one would at first suppose. Second, the simplicity and lack of difficulty in the first few verses make this section a good place to include this discussion. After all, a good letter writer, especially if his message is very important, does not load his introductory paragraph with his most perplexing profundities. The substantial difficulties and greater need for explanation come soon enough. Then, third, an educated Christian should really know just a little bit about textual criticism. He is sure to be confronted with objections to Christian doctrine that are based on these points.

Finally, the ordinary Christian, to whom this commentary is addressed, is urged to be patient and pay attention. It will be necessary to examine short phrases and even single words with care. The reader therefore runs the risk of not seeing the forest because of the numerous leaves. This is especially true in the first dozen verses. They are like practicing the scales of exegesis. The symphony begins

Preface

with verse 13 or 14. Not only must the reader look closely at translations given here; but he must look back at them, and other translations, as he proceeds through the discussion. One piece of advice, above all others, must be followed: always keep the Bible open before you; never shut it for a minute; otherwise you will be lost. The text is the word of God, and God requires your best efforts.

The First Chapter

1:1,2. Paul, apostle of Christ Jesus by the will of God, and Timothy our brother, to the saints in Colosse, brethren who believe in Christ: Grace to you and peace from God our Father and the Lord Jesus Christ.

Paul signs himself—in ancient letters the signature comes, as is more logical, at the beginning rather than at the end—as an apostle. In Galatia a strong clique vigorously attacked Paul's claim to be an apostle and it was necessary in his letter to the Galatians to defend his authority as well as his gospel. There also seems to have been painful opposition to Paul's apostleship in Corinth, as both epistles reveal; but it does not follow that any doubts or animosity in Colosse necessitated the word *apostle* in this case. The motive here, as in Romans, may have been that Paul had never visited these places (cf. 2:1) and so had to identify himself. The salutation in Romans, and especially in the two letters to Timothy and the one to Titus, show that it is a simple statement of fact: an important fact to be sure, for an apostle received gifts, bore responsibilities, and exercised an authority that other Christians never did. There is no basis in the New Testament for supposing that apostolic authority was transferred to a line of popes. If it were not for the historic connotation of the phraseology, one could accept a sort of "apostolic succession," in that earlier generations of Christians baptized later generations, and even that earlier pastors ordained those who followed. But sacramentarianism, three orders of clergy, and in particular a *Pontifex Maximus* with a triple tiara are foreign to the original Christianity of the New Testament.

Verse one further states that Paul was an apostle by the will of God. Romans 1:1 says that God called and separated him. I Corinthians, II Corinthians, I and II Timothy make similar claims. In Paul, Jesus' words, "Ye have not chosen me, but I have chosen you," are strikingly exemplified. That Paul was made an apostle by the will of God does not seem surprising in view of his extraordinary and spectacular conversion. But one must remember that all Christians have been called and separated by the will of God, no matter how ordinary and unspectacular their conversion may have been. It is always God who turns, or converts.

Paul, joining Timothy to himself, sends the letter to the saints in Colosse. The two words, *sainted* and *faithful*, or *holy* and *faithful*, look like parallel adjectives. But this parallelism produces a disturbing translation; viz., "to those in Colosse, both the holy and the faithful." This would suggest that some in Colosse were neither holy nor faithful, to whom therefore Paul did not address the letter. This connotation can be avoided by noting that the plural of *sainted* or *holy* is usually not an adjective but a noun in Paul's letters. Therefore, the translation will be, "to the saints in Colosse, the brethren who believe in Christ."

That the noun *saints* has a definite New Testament (especially a Pauline) meaning makes it superfluous to say "saints in Christ." The word *saint* by itself includes that idea. Therefore, as the argument will shortly show, "in Christ" is better taken as the object of the saints' belief.

In English the word *saint* has come to connote not merely good character, but morality of an exceptional degree. This linguistic development causes confusion. Following the lead of the Old Testament, we could better translate the word as *devoted, consecrated, set apart*, the last two of which do not emphasize moral excellence. In circumcision and in baptism children are *dedicated* to God; but sometimes, unfortunately, the dedication does not result in a "dedicated" life. At any rate, the word *saint* refers to any and every Christian; and this is how Paul uses it. Surely it is not unreasonable to assume that Paul sent his letter to all the Christians in Colosse. They were all saints and believers. Therefore, the translation "faithful brethren in Christ" at best obscures the sense. We cannot be sure how "faithful" they were, nor do we know to what degree of sanctification some of them had attained. But we can be sure that they believed.

That they all were saints because they were believers receives support from Romans 1:7 and other passages where Paul evidently includes all the membership. It requires no papal canonization to become a saint. This point has a further implication. In referring to Paul we may properly use his title and call him the Apostle Paul. But to refer to him as "Saint Paul" is no mark of distinction, for all within God's church are saints. For this reason too, the expression "Saint Paul" is a concession to Romanism. All Christians are saints, however unsaintly we sometimes behave. The Colossians whom Paul addressed were saints because they all were brethren who believed in Christ.

So much for the word *saints*. Now the word *believers*.

Some commentators object to the translation "the brethren who believe in Christ." They have two reasons. First, the word in question is not a participle, i.e., "who believe"; it is an adjective and should be translated *faithful*. Second, the preposition *en*, "in" Christ, does not indicate Christ as an object of belief, but rather refers to the Christians' incorporation into the body of Christ. A spiritual union, not an object of belief, is the idea.

This view is not without merit. But neither is it altogether convincing. As for the preposition *en*, instead of *eis*, "into," or *epi*, "upon," we shall see that it has several meanings. Surely in verse 4 it means faith in Christ. In addition to the connotations of Greek prepositions, if the idea were that of a spiritual union, the word *pistois* would be superfluous. Simply "brethren in Christ" would be quite enough. Therefore it makes better sense, to the present commentator at least, to take Christ as the object of their belief.

The salutation, similar to those in all the Pauline epistles, requires little explanation as regards its meaning. One point alone needs emphasis. At various times in church history and in some localities, a subjective type of mind has claimed to be superior in spirituality. This "pietism" has found representatives in the late twentieth century. They put emphasis on the intensity of believing and minimize the object of belief. In some cases the object virtually disappears. "Guilt-feelings" are a cause of concern, while guilt is rather ignored. The New Testament is more objective. Just as *grace* is the favor bestowed by God on his people, so too *peace* is not any subjective "peace of mind" but an objective peace with God. We were once his enemies; now God has established peace. It is this objective peace with God that Paul asked God to bestow on the Colossians.

Aside from the meaning of the salutation there is a slight textual problem, which is of some small interest, even though, like most textual problems, it hardly affects the meaning. Some manuscripts read, at the end of the verse, "from God our Father." Other manuscripts have, "from God our Father and the Lord Jesus Christ." The latter reading has as good, and perhaps even slightly better manuscript evidence in its favor. However, many commentators and editors think a scribe added the words later to conform the wording to Pauline usage. But why could not Paul himself use Pauline usage?

The preface to this commentary, a few pages ago, suggested a connection between textual criticism and evangelistic endeavor. Evangelistic endeavor is not and should not be restricted to mammoth crusades. The more effective form consists of an individual Christian explaining the gospel message to an unregenerate friend. If educated, both of them have probably heard some rumors that scribes altered the original text, until as Bultmann extremely says, "We do not know a single thing Jesus ever said or did." Such doubts are psychological hindrances to the acceptance of the gospel by an unregenerate person, as they are also disturbing factors in the mind of the Christian. The example just given does not aim to induce the reader to become a professional textual critic: that would require a lot of Greek and much other information as well. Its aim is to serve as an example—an example, if one be permitted a little exaggeration, of triviality. Most of the textual variations are as trivial as this one. The meaning is the same no matter which reading one selects.

To be sure, there are a few that alter the sense, but not very many. With this knowledge the Christian himself will be free from disturbing doubts, and he can meet the instructed or usually uninstructed objections of his secular friend.

While we are on the subject, a few other items of information can be added, and then they need not be repeated later. Unlike Plato's dialogues and Aristotle's works, which come to us in eight, twelve, or less than twenty manuscripts, the New Testament survives in nearly five thousand—not all of which are complete. Obviously, if a thousand scribes copy an original, there will be more variations than twenty scribes would make. Roughly there is in the New Testament one variation in every eight words. Counted in this number is such a variation as Jesus Christ—Christ Jesus. Variants that affect the meaning are about one in a thousand words. Therefore, our texts of the New Testament are established with far greater certainty than the texts of Plato and Aristotle. This is good to know when confronted with unbelief.

These remarks on textual criticism are obviously brief and inadequate. The subject is intensely interesting, and even without a knowledge of Greek an inquiring Christian can easily read up on it with pleasure and profit. But the subject of the present book is Colossians, not textual criticism.

1:3. We give thanks to God, Father of our Lord Jesus Christ, always for you as we pray....

The plural, "we give thanks" is not to be regarded as an editorial "we." Verse 1 is so close that the "we" includes Timothy. Later, in verse 23, Paul pointedly speaks in the singular. Here Paul speaks for Timothy also.

Paul uses the plural *we* because Timothy is associated with him. Note, however, that Paul, who has just claimed to be an apostle, when he imposes binding obligations on the Colossians, though he has never seen them, uses the singular. Verse 25 again asserts his apostleship, and chapter 2 contains some exhortations or directions.

Now, for the sense of the verse: "We give thanks ... always ...

pray." Since the word *always* stands between the two verbs, one wonders to which it belongs.

The absence of punctuation in Greek manuscripts sometimes leaves us in doubt regarding connections between two words. In this verse the word *always* can be connected with "we give thanks," in spite of the several words that separate them. The verse would then say, "We always give thanks for you when we pray." Or it could mean, "We give thanks, praying for you always." Another uncertainty is the relation of "for you." Did Paul *give thanks* for the Colossians, or did he *pray* for the Colossians?

Eadie (*in loc.*) suggests that the Colossians did not need to be told that Paul prayed for them; but they would be encouraged by knowing that he always gave thanks for them.

This too is a trivial difference. Fortunately such a trivial difference comes early in the epistle. Unencumbered with disturbing doctrinal consequences, it is a good example of what is meant by construing the text. The reader must decide whether a word should be connected with what precedes or what succeeds. Every so often the absence of punctuation leaves it unclear where a sentence ends. The period may be placed before or after a complete clause. Thus two interpretations are equally possible so far as mere grammar is concerned. The decision depends on fitting the phrase into Paul's argument.

1:4,5.   ... having heard of your faith in Christ Jesus and the love which you have to all the saints because of the hope stored up for you in heaven, which you previously heard about in the word of the truth of the gospel...

This sentence does not end at verse 3, but continues through verse 8. Paul often wrote long complicated sentences. He here explains how he can give thanks for the Colossian Christians. Such an explanation is in order because Paul had not founded this congregation and knew very few, if any, of them. His thanksgiving depends therefore on the good reports he has heard about them. Perhaps their faith was not spoken of throughout the whole world, as the faith of the Romans was; but, nonetheless, their faith in Christ and their love toward all other Christians was commendable.

As with verse 2, some commentators, even here in verse 4, wish to see some sort of spiritual incorporation (a contradictory phrase, if there ever was one) rather than the object of belief. But here even more clearly than in verse 2, the latter idea is obvious. Various prepositions can follow the idea of belief. One cannot properly say that *eis* or *epi* must be used. One can better argue that this verse demonstrates that *en* is quite possible.

The word *pistis* means faith, and the verses commentators cite to make it mean faithfulness do not always prove their point.[1] For example, in Matthew 8:10, 9:2, and 9:22 the people who had *faith*, had had no time to be *faithful*. Faithfulness takes a long time, faith does not. The woman touched the hem of his garment because she *believed* something about the nature and power of Christ; not because she had discharged many obligations faithfully. Her faith is called great because she was so thoroughly convinced of the truth she believed. Just as clear are Matthew 9:28–29 (cf. Matthew 16:28). Matthew 21:21, contrasting faith with doubt, also allows no time for faithfulness. Even Matthew 23:23, where faith might seem to mean long obedience, the fact that the matters of obedience are mentioned separately might indicate that faith is an additional factor. In this regard, note that the Pharisees did not *believe* Moses (John 5:46–47). They were not the fundamentalists of Christ's day; they were the modernists. The Sadducees were outright humanists.

In view of the nineteenth- and twentieth-century vogue of the

---

1. This type of anticreedal objection is more vigorously leveled against the Old Testament. The Hebrew word, say some commentators, means faithfulness or firmness, and not belief. When it is pointed out to them that the LXX translators, who used Hellenistic Greek, used the word *pisteuō*, they lamely reply that the Alexandrian rabbis were "obviously embarrassed." James Barr, a scholar of unquestioned heterodoxy, writes, "The unwillingness of much modern theology [in contrast with the 'fundamentalist' type thinking] to admit that belief or faith can be properly be given to a saying or words, or its tendency to insist that such belief in something said is totally different in kind from faith understood as a relationship with a person, may also affect the exegesis here" (*The Semantics of Biblical Language*, pp. 172ff.). The *here* in the last sentence means that Torrance allows his modernism to control his exegesis.

universal brotherhood of man and the universal fatherhood of God, it is worth noting that Paul does not mention a universal love, but a love toward all the saints. No doubt a Christian is under obligation to do good to all men, but the Christian is a citizen of Augustine's City of God, not of the other city.

The reason for their faith and love lies in the hope stored up for them in heaven. Paul frequently gives reasons for his statements. It is enlightening, when reading his epistles, to note words like *for, since, because,* and other connectives. Skipping over them carelessly allows the truth to escape. Here the faith and love of the Colossians are based on a hope stored up for them in heaven. It is not their subjective hoping that causes their faith, not an activity in their mind and heart, but a blessed reward or inheritance in heaven. The word *inheritance* does not occur at this point. It is found later in verse 12. The name of the thing hoped for is not given here. But though not named, it is clearly something objective, stored up for them in heaven. Obviously their subjective hoping is not stored up in heaven. It is a present activity in their own hearts and minds.

This inheritance, this hope, this heavenly store, they had previously heard about, previous to Paul's writing. What they heard was "the word of the truth of the gospel," which Epaphras had preached to them. Note that the gospel, the inheritance, the hope was preached; and for this reason also could not be their subjective hoping.

The wording "the word of the truth of the gospel" sounds clumsy in English. Ephesians 1:13 has a similar, though clearer, phrase: "the word of truth, the gospel of your salvation." These phrases are not to be taken to mean "the true gospel," as if distinguishing it from some inaccurate account of the gospel. Even a Christian can speak of "the true doctrine of Hinduism," if he wishes to correct a mistaken account of that religion. What Paul emphasizes here, on the contrary, is that the gospel is true, as even the most accurate account of Hinduism is not. The gospel, the good news, the doctrine (word) is the doctrine of truth. God is the God of truth; if we know the truth, the truth will set us free; as Jesus said, "Sanctify them through the truth—thy word is truth." This truth is what the Colossians believed.

1:6–8 [The gospel] which is present to you, as it is also in all the world, producing fruit and increasing as also in you, from the day you heard it and knew the grace of God in truth; as you learned it from Epaphras our beloved co-slave, who is faithful on your behalf, a deacon of Christ, who also explained to us your love in the Spirit.

Here is the end of the complicated sentence, these final clauses of which also present some choices among shades of meaning.

The first clause, "which is present to you," is usually translated "which came to you." The verb ordinarily means *to be present*; but a derivative meaning is *come*. The preposition "to" perhaps favors *come* rather than *be present*. After *be present*, one might expect the preposition *with* instead of *to*. On the other hand, the next clause has *in*, and this favors *be present* rather than *come*: "as it is also [present] in all the world."

The two *also's* should be noted as well. The first impression is one of parallelism: both *in you* and *in all the world* have the same result, namely, producing fruit and increasing. These two participles then must be in apposition with *the gospel* in the preceding verse. It is the gospel that produces fruit and increases both in the world and in you. This parallelism is a consideration hard to disallow. "Just as," repeated twice, is a rather emphatic comparative.

However, the New American Standard version, and other translations, break the parallelism and reject the apposition, no doubt because the two participles, "bearing fruit and increasing" are nominative or accusative and not genitive as *the gospel* is. Thus it would read: "the gospel which has come to you [comma] just as in all the world also it is constantly bearing fruit and increasing." This hardly makes much sense; but it must be admitted that there is some awkwardness either way you take it.

There follows another "just as": "bearing fruit and increasing [in the world] just as also in you." This effect of preaching the word of truth has continued from the day the Colossians first heard it and understood the grace of God in truth. There is no difficulty in construing the words of this clause; but its meaning escapes some people who think themselves very devout. Contrary to the emotion-alism of the Pentecostals, contrary to a quieter pietism, and as well contrary to the Neo-orthodox or dialectical encounter that annihi-lates two thousand years of time in the crisis of a moment, the gospel is information, good news, truth. It is something *heard*, something to be *known* or understood. The grace of God comes in or by *truth*. It is something to be *learned*. As the Puritans used to say, Chris-tianity is taught, not caught. It was Epaphras who had taught the Colossians. They *learned* the gospel from him. Any denigration of the meaning, the intellectual content, the truth, of the good news is a rejection of the gospel itself.

Epaphras was Paul's "beloved fellow-bond-slave," a faithful ser-vant or deacon of Christ. *Deacon* and *servant* are the same word. Originally it meant any kind of servant, and it frequently bears this general meaning in the New Testament. Sometimes, however, it is used as a technical term to denote a special office to which elected officials are ordained.

Epaphras is called a *faithful* servant. Since the two words follow-ing *faithful* are *on your behalf*, faithful is a better translation than believing. To say that Epaphras was a believer for their sakes does not make good sense. Here for once *pistos*, the adjective, has a subjective reference.

Epaphras may have been the one who founded the Colossian church. Here he has explained to Paul their love in (the) spirit. This phrase could mean, so far as grammar goes, that the love referred to was the work of the Holy Spirit. But since the context contains no other reference to the Holy Spirit, the grammar also allows a weaker sense: your spiritual love, or even, the love that exists in your (mind and) spirit. The same point occurs in the next verse also.

This is where the introduction ends. The Epistle to the Colossians cannot be outlined with the same logical precision as the Epistle to the Romans. We may, however, clearly consider verses 1 and 2 as the salutation, and less clearly verses 3 through 8 as an introductory paragraph. Then, although verses 9–23 are clearly a single con-nected paragraph, there is, in the middle of a sentence, a distinct break in the subject matter. We might call verse 14 a connecting verse, but in any case everything before it directly concerns the

Colossian Christians, and everything after it explains the nature and work of Christ.

> 1:9. Therefore we also, from the day we heard it, do not cease praying for you and beseeching [God] to fill you with the knowledge of his will in all wisdom and spiritual understanding...

Calvin makes a remark on this verse which seems to go beyond what the verse really says, at least if the verse is not enlarged by other passages. Further, it takes us somewhat far afield, however important it may be in its own right. Therefore let us dispose of Calvin's remark before proceeding with the usual commentary. Calvin says, "'In all wisdom;' by which he [Paul] means that the will of God, of which he has spoken, was the only rule of right knowledge."

This bears on the scope of apologetics. Apologetics is a difficult subject. Thomas Aquinas, William Paley, and others have held that the existence of God can be demonstrated by a series of valid syllogisms starting with the data of sensation. Their proofs obviously depend on the possibility of knowing something about the physical universe; that is, they depend on a certain amount of scientific knowledge. This knowledge is not obtained from God's written revelation, but from laboratory experiment. Other apologists not only deny that the syllogisms in question are valid, but also take a skeptical view of science. Calvin seems here to limit knowledge, or right knowledge, to what may be deduced from the assertions of Scripture. Scripture is the only rule of right knowledge. Calvin is not willing to designate the changing theories of science as knowledge. Calvin may indeed be right. But this verse by itself does not prove that he is. Let us therefore see precisely what the verse says.

The apostle Paul was a very logical thinker. He takes care to show the relationships among his ideas. Verse 9 begins with *therefore*. What then is the connection between this verse and what precedes? Try the possibilities. It is not so much a matter of Greek syntax, but of logical connection. Did Paul pray for the Colossians *because* Epaphras told him about them? This makes good sense, for if Paul had never heard of the Colossians, or if knowing there was such a city, but not knowing of any Christians there, he could not have prayed for them. This interpretation also has the advantage of making the connection with the nearest preceding clauses, viz., verses 7 and 8.

Even if you wish to find the reason for Paul's prayers in the Colossians' faith and love, verse 4 also mentions the report Epaphras brought to Paul.

Incidentally, however one construes verse 3, and whether one connects the *always* with prayer or with thanksgiving, here at least Paul prays always.

The phrase "from the day we heard it" may be a stylistic nicety echoing the words in verse 6. Paul is not very strong on stylistic niceties. As noted earlier, his sentences are heavy and complicated; but always logical.

So, Paul prayed continually for the Colossians. The content of his, and Epaphras', prayers deserve particular notice. Their request to God is that he fill them with the knowledge of his will. What one should notice is the emphasis on knowledge. Some commentators, Alford for example, making too much of etymology, insist that here is a very strong word for knowledge: the word *knowledge* compounded with the preposition *upon*; whereas the uncompounded word, just simply *knowledge*, is a weaker word. That Paul throughout the epistle emphasizes knowledge cannot be doubted. Indeed this is a point that needs emphasis in our pragmatic, antiintellectual age. But so frequent is Paul's emphasis on knowledge that one need not resort to irrelevant etymologies. Actually, New Testament usage evinces little or no difference between the two terms. Of course the knowledge here in view is not a knowledge of botany or astronomy, but a knowledge of God's will. One commentator (A.S. Peake, *in loc.*) wishes to restrict the knowledge of God's will to knowledge of moral principles. That moral principles are included is quite clear in verse 10; but verse 9 is more inclusive. The knowledge of his will must certainly be the whole counsel of God, as Paul indicates in Acts 20:27. He would not make a truncated knowledge the ideal for the Colossians. Nor for us today, either. This idea of the greatest possible knowledge is emphasized by the phrase "in all wisdom." The commentator just mentioned in disagreement nevertheless allows that *wisdom* "embraces the whole range of mental faculties," and *understanding* "is the special faculty of intelligence or insight which discriminates between the false and the true." Thus Paul, like John in his Gospel, emphasizes truth. Mere feelings and fleeting emotions cannot compare with absolute, unchanging, eternal truth. To repeat, in order to avoid all careless misunderstanding, Paul is not referring to botany or astronomy. He is speaking of the will of God, and hence writes "in all wisdom and spiritual understanding"; or equally correct, "in all spiritual wisdom and understanding."

Paul does not recommend a minimal, superficial knowledge. As he says elsewhere (I Cor. 3:2; Heb. 5:12, 13), milk may be fine for newborn babes, but mature men need strong meat. So here he does not prescribe a teaspoonful before meals. He wants us to be *full* of *all* wisdom and understanding.

One of the great twentieth-century tragedies in the church is that so many, not lay members only, but ministers in particular, are satisfied to know so little. A disappointing, though not unexpected result of a questionnaire to ministers in a certain large American city, showed a very small percentage used the Greek they learned in seminary. Some seminaries do not even teach Greek, and they replace theology with sociology.

Herbert M. Carson (*in loc.*) expresses a less extreme, but equally erroneous, viewpoint: we "should not be misled into thinking that their [the Colossians'] goal is a barren orthodoxy. Hellenistic Judaism may content itself with an intellectual growth in religious knowledge divorced from life." This sentence misrepresents Hellenistic Judaism and Christianity as well. Neither Hellenistic Judaism nor even pagan Greek philosophy divorced knowledge from life. The Stoics and Epicureans, whom Paul mentioned in Acts 17:18, were primarily ethical philosophers. Their interest in physics was secondary. The Jews before Philo, Philo himself, and even more so the movement that resulted in the Talmud and Midrash were strongly ethical, and the latter were even casuistic. They insisted on a very strict standard of living. The trouble with the Judaizers and the later Jews was not their divorce of religious knowledge from life, but the fact that their ethical theory was not Christian.

Christianity also obligates us to certain norms of morality. But without the intellectual orthodoxy, the Ten Commandments cannot be defended.

It may be worth a paragraph to consider the two words *wisdom* and *understanding* (comprehension, intelligence, insight). Peter Lombard, without much insight, connected wisdom with the contemplation of eternal truth and understanding with the study of the invisible attributes of the Creator and his creatures. Others make *wisdom* theoretic and *understanding* practical, though this seems backwards. Eadie (*in loc.*) remarks that those who make them synonymous are "too slovenly to be in accordance with accurate philology." It seems to the present commentator that they are synonymous.

We shall see later (2:8) what Paul thinks of secular learning. Here he advocates the knowledge of the Spirit-inspired Scripture, for it is in Scripture alone that we can learn the whole counsel of God.

1:10. . . [so as] to walk worthily of the Lord, toward all pleasing, in every good work, bearing fruit and increasing in the knowledge of God. . .

Although the knowledge of God in the previous verse cannot be limited to the commands of morality, the knowledge is designed to promote morality. We must try to please the Lord in all things. The translation above is awkward, but the phrase "toward all pleasing" is a faithful reproduction of Paul's wording. Its meaning cannot be mistaken because the next two clauses define it. We are required to do every good work. Good works are those prescribed by the Ten Commandments and their implications as given in all the precepts throughout the Bible.

In the history of the church, every so often, groups emerge that consider an emphasis on God's commands as legalistic and non-Christian. "Free from the law," they sing, "O blessed condition: I can sin as I please and still have remission." What these people do with chapters 6, 7, and 8 of Romans is hard to understand. Here in Colossians Paul urges us to every good work, producing fruit and growing in the knowledge of God.

In verse 6 above it was the gospel that produced fruit and increased. Here the same two participles (now masculine, not neuter) attach to the Colossian Christians. That is to say, Paul prays that God may grant increase of knowledge to the Colossians. And with this, the New Testament emphasis on knowledge also increases.

Contrasted with those who hold the law in contempt are others who, rightly enough, condemn murder, adultery, and theft, and stress holy actions: but here they stop; and this, however, is not enough. The text speaks of "every good work." Now, morality is indispensably important. But not all good works have the form of external action. It is no invitation to steal, if one insists on internal good works—on thinking correctly. In this verse the words say, "growing in the knowledge of God." In the previous verse Alford may have made a nonexistent distinction between *gnosis* and *epignosis*; but here he makes the admirable remark, "It is the knowledge of God which is the real instrument of enlargement, in soul and life, of the believer." The knowledge of God goes by the name of theology. Any man, exemplary in external rectitude, is still not a mature Christian unless he advances in theology. Avoidance of fornication and theft, however essential, is not a substitute for an understanding of the Trinity. This is a verse with which to confront the antiintellectuals.

> 1:11.   ... being empowered with all power according to the might of his glory to all perseverance and patience, with all gladness...

The complicated sentence continues. It began with verse 9 and does not end until verse 17.

The participle *being empowered*, through the two participles in the previous verse, refers back to the Colossians, last mentioned as such in verse 2. In such long sentences it is easy to forget what is going on. Verse 11 does not say that the Colossians are empowered with all power; the phrase depends particularly on verse 9 as one of the petitions of Paul's prayer. Paul beseeches God to give them strength, great strength, reflective of the divine glory. And for what

27

purpose? Perhaps, in some cases, for stedfastness in the face of persecution and martyrdom; but more usually for stedfastness in the face of ridicule, minor harassment, and even the daily difficulties of living. The usual, even the normal, Christian life is not one of heroics. To illustrate: a brilliant and vigorous chess player aims at surprising combinations that result in a sudden checkmate at move 22; but his equally brilliant opponent patiently plays for position, foils the combinations, and wins at move 61.

Before continuing with "patience" it is well to note "according to the might of his glory." Paul prays that we may be "empowered with all power according to the might of his glory." It does not seem sufficient to take this as "his glorious might." Something stronger seems to be suggested. Perhaps "the might which constitutes his glory" might do; but the best interpretation is "the might that is characteristic of his glory." By this might we are to be strengthened to all perseverance and patience (longsuffering) with joy.

The next two words are "with gladness," or "joyously." The New American Standard version connects the "joyously" with the next verse and makes it read, "all steadfastness and patience [comma] joyously giving thanks." This is probably a bad translation. As said before, a modern editor must insert punctuation marks as he sees fit, for there is none in the manuscripts. But it makes better sense (does it not?) to connect joy with patience, where it is needed. This is a point that can stand being pointed out. To speak of giving thanksgiving with joy is just a bit tautological.

> 1:12. ... giving thanks to the Father who has made you [or, us] fit for your share in the inheritance of the saints in light ...

The human nature with which we all are born is not fit to share in any heavenly inheritance. We are born guilty of Adam's original sin, and our own sins add to the guilt. But God makes us fit, for which we give humble and hearty thanks.

The words "in light" are a little puzzling. One commentator suggests: God fits you for the inheritance by means of the light of the gospel. This not only fits with the knowledge in verses 9 and 10, but also with the idea, in the following verse, of deliverance from the power of darkness. Light often symbolizes truth, and darkness, error. The trouble is that this interpretation divorces the saints from the light and connects it with the participle "fitted." This is surely awkward.

A second interpretation makes light symbolize righteousness, and darkness, sin. In this case God fitted us for our part in the inheritance of the saints who are now progressing in righteousness, having been rescued from their previous immorality. But since the Colossians are themselves saints, the phrase is tautological.

Or we may take it as the departed saints who now dwell in the light of heaven, full of glory. This seems in itself to be the best interpretation. It certainly conforms to the mention of the inheritance, for inheritance much more clearly designates heaven than it accords with our present condition.

If this be the meaning of verse 12, it rules out the ASV translation of verse 13.

1:13. . . . who rescued us from the power of darkness and transferred us into the kingdom of the Son of his love . . .

The NAS translation inserts the conjunction *for* at the beginning of this verse. Thus the present verse is taken as a reason for the previous verse: either we give thanks because God rescued us, or God fitted us because he rescued us. However, there is no such conjunction in the text. Verse 13 is not given as a reason for verse 12. True enough, God's transferring us into the kingdom could be a reason for thanksgiving. But it is not so stated. It is simply an additional fact; and this ties in very well with our understanding of the previous verse. Taking the phrase as a simple addition does not at all conflict with the contrast between the light of heaven and the darkness of our preregenerate condition.

More important is the identification of the kingdom into which God transfers us. Although the previous verse spoke of the light of heaven in which the departed saints now dwell, the kingdom cannot be identified with, that is, restricted to our future life in heaven. Nor does the term *kingdom* mean the millennium. One same reason makes both of these interpretations false. The reason is that God has already transferred us into the kingdom, whereas the millennium and heaven are both future. Christ is King now. Christ is our King now. As the Westminster Shorter Catechism says, "Christ executeth the office of King by subduing us to himself, ruling and defending us, and by restraining and conquering all his and our enemies." No doubt that "of his kingdom there shall be no end;" but its beginning is in the past, not the future.

1:14. ... in whom we have redemption, the forgiveness of sins...

At this point it is necessary to note the stages in Paul's thought. Grammatically these clauses are still dependent on Paul's prayer. But here and more clearly in the next verse the idea of prayer recedes and straightforward theological instruction begins. Verse 13 is the last in which the Colossians themselves appear; verse 14 is the transition; and the definite break comes with verse 15, even though the latter continues the same long sentence.

Very well; the verse says, "in whom we have redemption." The Greek preposition *en* frequently means *by*. This really makes better sense here. Christ is the agent of our redemption—he accomplished it. If anyone prefers the usual translation *in*, it must be understood in a metaphorical sense, difficult to explain. A. S. Peake argues, "not *by* whom, but *in* whom; if we possess Christ we possess *in* him our deliverance." This of course begs the question. What Peake has done is to define the word *in* by the word *in*. What he should have done is to explain how deliverance can be in Christ, as in a room, rather than by Christ as an agent. Therefore *by* is better.

The word *redemption* signifies a deliverance by means of paying a ransom. Sometimes the context does not explicitly mention a ransom—the means of deliverance is left unexpressed; but this indeterminateness is by no means a denial of the idea of ransom.

The First Chapter of Colossians

Thayer's *Lexicon* has "to redeem one by paying the price . . . a releasing effected by payment of ransom . . . everywhere in the NT metaph., viz., deliverance effected through the death of Christ from the retributive wrath of a holy God and the merited penalty of sin. . . . "

Thayer's paragraph can hardly be called a translation of the word *apolutrōsis*; but it is a fine statement of the New Testament idea.

Unbelieving New Testament scholars have often tried to eradicate this idea. One of them bases his rejection on the next words of this verse, viz., "the forgiveness of sins," a phrase he regards as the definition of redemption. His argument seems to depend on the assumption that forgiveness and ransom are incompatible concepts. But this is not a logical argument. First, "the forgiveness of sins" may be only a part of the definition. Surely redemption includes sanctification and glorification as well as forgiveness. There may also be other parts, among which an act of ransom may be found. Then, second, as far as grammar is concerned, appositive clauses are not necessarily even a part of a definition. One can say, "Baseball, the great American game. . . ." This neither defines nor describes baseball. Hence the argument above is fallacious.

Now, we may be inclined to think that *forgiveness* is more than an accidental apposition. It may well be a part of the definition. No matter: even if it were the complete definition, which it is not, still the definition alone would say nothing concerning the means by which redemption is accomplished. Suppose redemption were precisely the forgiveness of sins; the forgiveness could still be motivated by the suffering and merits of Christ. We must insist that Christ gave his life a ransom for many.

At this point we come to the main transition in Paul's thought—the transition from a prayer for the Colossians to an explanation of the person and nature of Christ who redeemed us.

The sentence as such began at verse nine, and with the help of participles and relative pronouns continues to the end of verse 17. But the first two-thirds of the sentence gives the contents of Paul's prayers for the Colossians and somewhat reflects their spiritual development. If not verse 14, certainly verse 15 begins to describe the person and work of Christ. A neat outline is hard to produce because toward the end of the chapter, say from verse 23 on, the subject returns to the Colossians again and Paul's concern for them.

> 1:15. ... who is the image of God invisible, the first-born of all creation...

Now we have arrived at the most difficult and the most profound theme in the epistle. Indeed it might well be called the most profound theme in all the New Testament. This is Jesus Christ himself: more particularly who and what Christ is.

The difficulty for the Colossians was much greater than it is for us. We are the heirs of two thousand years of theological study. With this advantage we pursue our exegesis and theological systematization. We have known all about the crucifixion from our youth up. It is an old story and we take it much for granted. But for the Colossians the idea of a crucified redeemer was altogether new and most perplexing. Though they lived in a remote village, remote both from Jerusalem and from Rome, they were Greek-speaking Romans, and to them such claims for a crucified criminal were as absurd and repulsive as the idea of a crucified Messiah was to the Jews.

However, if we stop and think, the advantage in time that we have over the Colossians fades before a difficulty that all ages must face. C. A. F. Moule (*in loc.*, pp. 58–59) speaking of the claim in this verse, that Jesus is the image of God and the first-born of all creation, tellingly remarks, "... these stupendous words apply ... to one who ... had been crucified. The identification of that historical person—the Nazarene who had been ignominiously executed—with the subject of this description is staggering, and fairly cries out for some explanation."

What makes it staggering is the character and nature Paul ascribes to this man. Even if he had not been executed as a criminal, had he on the contrary been an honorable and respected prophet, priest, or king, it would have been not much less staggering to say or think these things about him. First, Paul says that Jesus is the image of God invisible (cf. II Cor. 4:4). Of course, this in itself is not too staggering. The term *image* denotes likeness and similarity; but the

32

degree of likeness can be defined, not by the word in isolation, but only by the context. As a matter of fact in I Corinthians 11:7 Paul asserts that man, any man, is the image and glory of God. We shall return to the word *image* in a moment; but let us first note the term *God*. The second half of the verse speaks particularly of Christ; but the first half speaks of God. The image is the image of God the invisible. God's invisibility is of some importance. The Children's Catechism—which little tots of four to eight, before the generation gap took over, used to memorize in preparation for memorizing the Shorter Catechism between the ages of eight to twelve—had a question, What is God? The answer was, "God is a spirit and has not a body like men." Things that are visible and tangible we call bodies. Humanistic secularism, the naturalism of Ernest Nagel, logical positivism, Dewey's behaviorism, all hold that only bodies are real and that God, spirits, and souls do not exist. The Bible, and in particular the Epistle to the Colossians, says a good deal about God and spirits. God is spirit, not body; he is neither visible nor tangible; and that is why it is idolatry to make graven images of him. Not only graven images: Numbers 33:52 forbids pictures as well. It is hard to see any Christian principle that allows us to put a picture of Christ in our wallet and carry it around in our hip pocket with our driver's license. God is spirit, and those that worship him must not genuflect before visible objects.

But if there can be no images or ikons of God, how can a man, even Christ, be the ikon of the invisible Father? To be sure the Greek word *eikon* means a picture; but it also means a phantom, a simile, a pattern, or any likeness. The likeness need not be something visible: a small town can be the governmental likeness of a larger city, and a son can be like his father or grandfather in vigor, determination or other moral qualities. Just because a boy is a chip-off-the-old-block does not mean we can cut him up with a penknife.

Christ's nature, qualities, characteristics therefore are the same as his Father's, and all invisible. Obviously Paul does not here refer to the bodily qualities of Christ received with his incarnation. But if we ask about his psychological qualities, we face a problem. Must we find the image only in Christ's pre-incarnate state, so that psychological as well as bodily qualities would be excluded from the image; or may we in some way find the image during his days on earth? But if the latter, are all of these psychological characteristics, or some only, constituents of the image? Clearly his sensations of hunger and fatigue could not be his similarity to God, for God neither sleeps nor grows weary.

Even the pre-incarnate image has its difficulties. These do not bother Hodge, Warfield, you, or me; but they embarrass Jehovah's Witnesses, Arius, and the Colossians. Those of us who follow Athanasius, in time and in thought, have solved the problem. If we already accept the deity of Christ, we go on. But Paul was writing to Hellenistic Romans who had first heard of the Old Testament, and of Jesus, only a little while before. It comes more easily for us today, but nevertheless we too must know his pre-incarnate characteristics, if we are to know who it was that became incarnate. It was the image of God invisible.

The subject, however, is a bit more complicated. If Paul's words can apply to the eternal Second Person, as indeed they do, the reference to the forgiveness of sins in the previous verse shows that Paul here has Jesus in mind. This therefore returns us to the question of the psychological qualities of the man Jesus. Jesus even during the days of his flesh was the image of God. The Gospel of John, probably written later than Colossians, records Jesus' words, "He that hath seen me hath seen the Father." This seeing was even less a matter of impressions on the retina than it was the fatigue and hunger inferred from such sense impressions. Rather it was the divine nature itself as the disciples grasped it, slowly and with difficulty, as in the case of Philip. "Believest thou not that I am in the Father, and the Father in me." Here the invisible God is "seen," not sensorily, but intellectually, in the incarnate Jesus.

The explanation is not yet complete, but to complete it we must go on to the next phrase—a phrase that seems to reduce considerably the orthodox conception of the eternal Son of God. The words are: "first-born of all creation." This seems to say that Christ is a created being, with a certain pre-eminence because first among created things, but created none the less. The previously mentioned bishop,

The First Chapter of Colossians

Arius, in the fourth century, maintained this view; and, as was also said before, Jehovah's Witnesses today hold precisely or substantially the same theory: Christ is the first angel God created. As an angel, Christ is spiritual like God, and therefore his image, and of a "similar substance." Arius was able, sometimes plausibly and sometimes not so plausibly, to interpret many New Testament phrases in support of his doctrine. It would be very profitable for many Christians today—profitable for learning the doctrine, profitable for refuting Jehovah's Witnesses, and profitable for strengthening the backbone of some pusillanimous Christians who fear the faces of heretics—to read Athanasius' defense of the full deity of Christ, as he stood, not only in the council, but also in the empire, "Athanasius *Contra Mundum*."

One argument against Arianism, not the only one by far and not even the best, comes in the very next verse; but let us first do as much as we can with the embarrassing phrase itself.

Would the kind reader patiently endure a few short paragraphs about the Greek word *prōtótokos*? It is true that this commentary is written mainly for church members who know no Greek. It is also true that for a great many matters the exegesis depends on the sense rather than on the ancient language. But the present word has caused so much debate that an intelligent reader wants to know something about it. Nor will a few Greek forms be so unintelligible as to leave him completely in the dark.

The word in question is *prōtótokos*, first-born, with the accent on the second syllable. The vowels in the word are an omega (a long *o*) and three omicrons (short *o*'s). A few commentators, in an effort to avoid the suggestion that Christ was the first among all created things, have argued that by putting the accent on the third syllable (second omicron) "first begotten" becomes "first begetter." Now, since the general rules of Greek accent do not usually fix the precise syllable on which it falls, and since the manuscripts have no accents at all, it is often possible to change the position of an editor's accentuation. However, the word, when it is made to mean first-begetter, is rather rare in Greek, and it is always feminine: it refers to a woman giving birth. A form of it is used for the virgin Mary, *theotokos*, translated as "Mother of God." Since the word is feminine, changing the accent in this passage is impossible. Christ is masculine.

To avoid the feminine noun, one might try to make use of the perfect participle of *prō-tiktō*, viz., *prōtetokos*. This won't work, however, because, in the first place, the second vowel in the participle is an epsilon, not an omicron; and, secondly, if the last vowel is an omicron, as it is in our text, and not an omega, the word is neuter, not masculine as the argument would require. Hence this emendation is impossible.

The word *prōtótokos*, the word in the verse, occurs eight times in the New Testament. The other seven instances help to fix its meaning here. Luke 2:7 refers to Jesus as Mary's firstborn son. Romans 8:29 says that God predestinated certain people to be conformed to the image of his Son, in order that the Son might be the firstborn among many brethren. Next comes the present verse, followed in verse 18 by "the firstborn of the dead." Hebrews 1:6 is, "When he again brings the firstborn into the world, he said, Let all the angels of God worship him." Hebrews 11:28: Moses "kept the Passover . . . so that he who destroyed the firstborn [of the Egyptians] might not touch them." Finally, Hebrews 12:23: The "church of the firstborn who are enrolled in heaven." These verses tell us that the word can be used literally, as in Luke, or with different shades of metaphorical meaning, as in the other seven instances. Christ therefore is the firstborn of all creation in some sense or other. What sense then makes the best sense?

In the Old Testament the firstborn's right of primogeniture is frequently mentioned. Since this concerns human affairs, there is the twofold sense of temporal priority and leadership or dominion. Arius applied both ideas to Christ. Since Christ was the first being God created, he had dominion over the beings God created later. But even in the Old Testament temporal priority is often enough missing. In Exodus 4:22 God says, "Israel is my firstborn." There was no secondborn. Literally and physically Israel was the secondborn and Esau was the first. Hence the meaning is not temporal priority but the legal rights of the boy whose father designates him as the head of the family. Exodus 4:22 refers to God's choosing a nation. Even though the next verse has the literal meaning, as God threatens to kill Pharaoh's firstborn son, the position of Israel as a nation is not one of temporal priority, but one of favor and privilege. Psalm 89:27 records the Lord's promise to or about David: "I will make him my firstborn, the highest of the Kings of the earth." Obviously this refers to office and dominion; not to any temporal priority, for David was neither the eldest child in his family, and all the more clearly he was not the first king who ever ruled on earth.

Therefore Paul's phrase, "the firstborn of all creation," at least *may* indicate dominion without any idea of temporal priority among created beings. Neither Arius, nor Jehovah's Witnesses who usually know little more than John 1:1 on the deity of Christ, can insist that the phrase *must* mean that Christ was the first created being.

Next come the words, "of all creation." Arius included Christ in "all creation." As the first created being, Christ was a part of creation. Just below in verse 18, Christ is the *prōtotokos* of the dead. Does not this mean that Christ was one of the dead and was the first to rise? The cases of Lazarus and the Old Testament resurrections do not count, for they were not permanent. Lazarus died again. Well, then Christ was the first member of a group to rise. So is He not the first member or part of a group that was created? Grammatically, therefore, "of all creation" would be a partitive genitive. Doubtless this is possible, but it is not necessary, even grammatically. There are other uses of the genitive besides the partitive use: for example, the genitive of comparison. In fact there is such an instance and usage in which the word *prōtos* is in the nominative. John 1:15 quotes John the Baptist as he defers to Jesus "because he was before me." The English obscures the point. When John the Baptist said, "He was before me," the word *before* is a nominative noun or adjective (prōtos), and *me* is genitive. It is hardly necessary to point out that "He was the first part of me" is nonsense. The genitive case is not always partitive. Hence the verse that is so taxing our patience, instead of meaning that Christ is the first part of creation, may mean that Christ is the Lord, ruler, or heir of creation. That it not only may, but does so mean, depends on the context.

Now, why is Christ the first begotten of all creation? Paul gives the reason immediately in the next verse, and this reason helps to clarify the meaning of the phrase that has been puzzling us. Christ is the firstborn of all creation *because* by him were created all the things in the heavens and on the earth. Now, if anything is clear, it is that a created being, a creature, cannot create anything. Nor is the creation in this verse limited to a few items. Even if it were, the creation of only one thing is still a work of omnipotence. Paul, however, is willing to emphasize the extent of the creation. Christ created all things, whether in the heavens or on the earth; whether visible or invisible; and whether thrones, lordships, or rulers. Christ therefore cannot be a part, even the first part of creation. He is the Creator.

There is another, even if lesser, consideration. If Paul had thought Christ to be the first of all created beings, he could have said so. The words would have been *prōtoktistos tōn pantōn ktismatōn*: "first created of all creatures." Paul did not say this. Christ is the firstborn, or heir; he is the Son of God. Now, it is true that all Christians are sons of God, as Arius insisted; but we are sons by adoption, and the nature of our sonship is quite different from the nature of the only begotten Son. In an effort to avoid the doctrine of eternal generation a recent theologian insisted that "only begotten" has no reference to begetting: it simply means "only." But reducing "only begotten" to "only" strengthens rather than weakens the argument, for it shows that the redeemed are not sons of God in the sense that Christ is. Christ is the only Son of God. The following verses strengthen this argument still more.

> **1:16.** ... **because by him were created all things in the heavens and on the earth, the visible things and the invisible things, whether thrones or lordships, or rulers, or authorities; the universe has been created by him and for him ...**

This sixteenth verse is conclusive against the idea that Christ was a created being. Meyer happily remarks that verse 16 is "the logically correct confirmation of *prōtotokos pasēs ktiseōs.*"

The First Chapter of Colossians

Christ was the Creator, and this refutes Arius because a created being cannot create. To emphasize Christ's role, Paul uses several words to describe the extent of his creative activity: it included all things, in heaven, on earth, visible, invisible, and so on. There is nothing left which Christ might not have created.

Something further needs to be said about Christ as Creator. Meyer is perverse and F. F. Bruce fuzzy in trying to substitute an ill-defined "in him" for the clear idea of agency expressed "by him." To quote F. F. Bruce: "It was 'in him' that all things were created. The preposition 'in' seems to denote Christ as the 'sphere' within which the work of creation takes place." Really, this language, "'sphere' within which," conveys no intelligible meaning. Bruce and Meyer both wish to deny that Paul teaches the doctrine of Philo that the Logos is God's blueprint of the physical world. It may easily be admitted that in these verses Paul does not teach that Christ is the intelligible archetype of the physical universe, or as Meyer says, the *causa exemplaris* according to which the *idea omnium rerum* was in Christ." But on this point two things should be kept in mind: first, the notion of agency does this as well as the unintelligible use of "sphere within which;" and, second, the argument is irrelevant and fallacious because though the doctrine Bruce does not like is not taught here, it may be taught somewhere else in the Bible. One must not insist that what Paul did not say here, he could not have said in another place. In fact, the doctrine Meyer rejects does not seem inconsistent with certain relevant passages of Scripture. Cannot an orthodox theologian hold that "the Son of God is the intelligible world, the *Kosmos noētos*"? How can this be avoided if Christ is the Logos and the Wisdom of God? Certainly, Christ's role as Logos in no way infringes on his agency in creation. Here in Colossians it is Christ's agency that is pointed out; not his role as Logos. This latter is found elsewhere. To repeat, Paul here asserts clearly and emphatically that Christ created the universe.

The emphasis comes in Paul's description of the created universe. The "all things," these objects, the realities, are not only the visible objects people ordinarily call things, but also invisible realities. Thrones and lordships in another context could refer to human political affairs. In Romans 13:1 *authorities* are human governments.

The First Chapter of Colossians

This is impossible here because, if it were so, the invisible realities would lack specification. Paul means superhuman spiritual beings.

One can suppose that the list gives a hierarchical order. Those beings called *thrones*, perhaps because Jewish and early Christian opinion pictured them as enthroned, may be the highest of created beings, while lordships indicate a lower order. But one should not suppose that this list must be exhaustive. Paul, rather than encouraging unfounded speculation concerning the rankings of angels, aims to impress his readers with the supremacy of Christ.

Incidentally none of these names for the ranking of angels is a Gnostic term. Therefore the view that Paul is here combatting the introduction of Gnosticism in the Colossian church must be held doubtful. Paul's phraseology does indeed or would indeed combat Gnosticism, if there had been any Gnosticism in Colosse to combat. Basilides and Valentinus described a spiritual world in which thirty eons or spiritual beings emerged from an Original Abyss of Silence. The last of the thirty, a beautiful girl named Sophia (wisdom or science), gave birth to or aborted the Christ. Clearly, therefore, this first Christ, after whom came many other Christs, could not have created the thirty eons. Hence Gnosticism and this verse are in stark contradiction. But Basilides and Valentinus lived about a century after Paul wrote to the Colossians; and there is no need of Gnosticism to stimulate Paul to record this revelation from God.

It is more likely, though that is not saying much, that Paul is opposing the Stoics and Epicureans. At least he acknowledges their existence in Acts 17:18; but this was in Athens not Colosse. However, even if he did not have these two schools in mind, since they both restricted reality to "matter," i.e., something that occupies space, Paul's words apply to them because he insists that spiritual entities are as real as physical objects, and indeed superior to them, for like God they are invisible.

Rather than searching for a conscious opposition to some first-century philosophy or religion, we might do better by taking this verse as a summation of the Old Testament teachings on angels.

The first superhuman spiritual being mentioned in Genesis, aside from God himself, was Satan, who had entered into a serpent. Evil spirits enter men and pigs in the Gospels. Next come the cherubim who guarded Eden with a flaming sword. Three mysterious beings appear to Abraham in Genesis 18, and two angels visit Lot in Sodom. Jacob saw angels in a dream. An angel encountered Balaam in Numbers 22. Judges 6 tells of the angel sent to Gideon. Satan appeared before God in Job. In Matthew, Satan incompletely quotes Psalm 91:11, "He shall give his angels charge over thee, to keep thee in all thy ways." David mentioned Michael, and Luke speaks of Gabriel. With this and more, Paul's interest in celestial beings is sufficiently accounted for without the Gnostic eons.

In I Corinthians 8:4 and 10:20 Paul asserts that idols are nothing, nor by implication Zeus, Poseidon, Ares, and the others; but, nevertheless, what the Greeks sacrifice, they sacrifice to demons.

Paul's immediate purpose in the Colossian epistle was to insist that Christ had created all those beings and that therefore he was superior to them. We today also need to inform people that Christ is the Creator of heaven and earth; but in addition, because of the naturalistic or humanistic secularism that dominates our culture, we must realize that they who are with us are more than they that be against us, for the encircling mountains are full of horses and chariots of fire. Would that God open our eyes to see through the twentieth century smog of secularism.

After naming these ranks of celestial spirits Paul adds, "The universe has been created by him and for him," that is, for his sake or for his purposes. Today even seemingly devout Christians entertain anthropocentric ideas. They think God made the world for them, rather than for himself. But Christianity is theocentric. They prefer to sing, "O how happy am I," instead of, "Glory to God in the highest." Even the words following this doxology are misunderstood: "... on earth peace, good-will toward men," or worse, "... peace to men of good will." What the angel actually sang, a little expanded, was, "... and on earth peace with God among those men on whom God bestows his sovereign pleasure." Theocentric religion does not forbid us from speaking of our own condition. The Psalms are full of personal reflections: "I will lift up mine eyes unto the hills..."; I "was glad when they said unto me...." But the phrases in Psalms 121 and 122 that follow these words show that their thought is centered on God. If we must emphasize one side over the other, let it be God's side.

Paul, however, is not focusing so much on God the Father as on God the Son. He repeats for emphasis that "the universe has been created by him and for his sake."

Sufficient has been said of Christ as the agent of creation at its beginning. Now something must be said about the purpose or end of creation. The world was not only created by him but also for him, for his sake, for his purposes, for his glory. He did not create the world for man's benefit. Man is part of the "all things" which Christ created for his own ends. More accurately perhaps, for his own end. This is a rebuke to those Christians who, no doubt unwittingly, entertain an anthropocentric theology instead of a theocentric theology. After World War II a certain resurgence of religion manifested itself in a bumper sticker which read "God is my co-pilot." What a compliment to God to make him a driver's or a pilot's equal!

1:17.   ... and he himself is before all [things] and by him the [whole] universe has been organized.

In verse 15 the priority insisted upon was a priority of rank. Any temporal idea, if present at all, was submerged. Here, on the contrary, a temporal priority is the point emphasized. If the universe was created and organized by him, there was a first moment for the universe, but no first moment for Christ. Strictly speaking a non-temporal eternity is not temporally prior to anything; but for us who are essentially temporal creatures it is hard to think and express the relation of time to eternity. So Paul says that Christ was before all things.

This again could have been a pointed denial of Gnosticism because in that system Christ comes last in the hierarchy of eons. But it is equally a denial of later Arianism, as also of some Jewish views which made the Messiah less than God. The phrase is a general exaltation of the Lord Jesus Christ and contradicts every differing theology.

The First Chapter of Colossians

This statement that Christ is before all things does not particularly refer to his pre-existence as it often appears in Christological discussions. A century ago orthodox theologians stressed the pre-existence of Christ in relation to his birth of the virgin Mary. A child was *born*, but a Son was *given*.

Now, it is important, very important, to insist that the person we call Jesus was not a new person who had just come into existence. You and I were not around a hundred years ago. But the person we call Jesus spoke to Abraham and Moses. "Abraham rejoiced to see my day; he saw it and was glad. . . . Before Abraham was, I am." But though we today must make clear to ignorant secularists (*heathen* is a better name) that Jesus left the ivory palaces to descend into this world of woe, the truth is already contained in the doctrine of the deity of Christ. If Jesus is God, of course His life did not begin in 6 B.C. or thereabouts. The reason it is necessary to talk about pre-existence is that many people are not very logical. It takes them a little time to figure out that if Jesus is God, he was there to talk to Abraham. Of course pre-existence does not require deity. Michael and Gabriel were alive in Abraham's day too; but this does not make them God. Deity implies pre-existence, but pre-existence does not imply deity. The phrase in question, verse 17 as a whole, does indeed imply Jesus' existence before 6 B.C.; but its explicit import is that he existed before Adam, before Michael, before all things.

The remainder of the verse is: ". . . and the universe was organized by him." *Ta panta* (all things) is the usual Greek phrase for the universe. The verb, however, needs some study. It can mean to come to grips with the enemy in battle, or to make an alliance with friends. It can mean to organize an army; to compose a book or poem; to make firm, prove, or establish; and even to be absorbed in thought. This information is not for the purpose of displaying the present writer's knowledge of Greek. Anyone who knows only so much as the alphabet can look up the word in a lexicon and read its meanings. Rather the purpose is to show that however important a knowledge of Greek is, there remains the necessity of an intelligent choice among several possibilities.

Now, the King James translators chose, "by him all things consist." The RSV says, "in him all things hold together." C. F. D.

43

The First Chapter of Colossians

Moule (*in loc.*) has the attractive phrase, "The universe owes its coherence to him." The present choice may not have Moule's literary finish, but it seems to be a bit clearer: ". . . by him the universe was organized." The outline of this organization is given in the first chapter of Genesis. But the climax of the paragraph, the crowning glory of Christ, is not the stars in their courses nor the microscopic mechanisms of the infinitesimal. Physical nature is but the backdrop and stage setting.

But before the culmination, let it be noted that the intricate sentence which began at verse 9 could end right here. The next verse, beginning with *and* could be a new sentence, running then to the end of verse 20. Of course, the word *and* does not necessitate a new sentence. It can simply continue the previous part. In this case, as a culmination of several verses, it even seems better to regard it so. In any case the sense is not altered.

> 1:18. . . . and he is the head of the body, the church;
> he is the princeps, the first-begotten of the dead, that
> he may himself have first place in everything . . .

There is a characteristic in this and the previous verse that has not yet been noted here. Ordinarily the Greek language does not use the pronoun *he* as the subject of a verb. Verbs in Greek have personal endings, and the endings make the pronoun unnecessary. *Eimi* in Greek means I am, as *sum* does in Latin. *Esti* does not mean simply *is*, but *he*, *she*, or *it is*. Despite this common usage, three times in this short passage, Paul uses the intensive pronoun *autos*. This unusual repetition places great emphasis on the person of Christ. Since the three instances of *autos* (he) are grammatically unnecessary, their appearance must have been deliberate. Hence the English translation could well sacrifice style for the same repetition: "he himself is before all things, . . . he himself is the head of the body . . . in order that he himself may have first place." The further fact that the oblique cases of this pronoun occur eight times in verses 16–20 makes the repetition all the more conspicuous.

These intensive pronouns seem to suggest that verse 18, or at least verses 18–19, are in some sense a culmination of the theme. The first point the verse makes is that Christ is the head of the church, and the church is His body. Paul uses the same figure of speech in Ephesians 1:22–23. This is a distinctly different metaphor from that in I Corinthians 12:21, where the head as much as the feet is a part of the body. When a given metaphor, with different meanings in different passages, is understood literally, confusion results. One must always seek the literal meaning which the figure of speech intends to adumbrate. The passage in I Corinthians gives rise to the idea that the church is an organism and not an organization. This is bad enough, but it is worse when Christ himself is made a particular part of that organism. Such a literal misunderstanding of figurative language may, in this latter half of the twentieth century, result from an irrational dislike of organization and "the establishment." Greater clarity of thought may be had by seeing how Merriam Webster's *Unabridged Dictionary* defines organisms. It lists four meanings. The first and fourth are essentially the same; so too are the second and third. These middle two are the most popular meaning of the term; namely, a living being with mutually dependent organs. The other, in brief, is any structure whose parts function in relation to each other. In this sense an automobile is an organism and so is a business corporation.

Those who insist that the church is a living organism obviously reject this latter meaning. They also ignore or minimize the Scriptural material that specifies how the visible manifestations of the invisible church must be organized. In their revolt against the establishment they have a poor opinion of deacons, elders, presbyters, general councils and all administrative and judicial functions. I am well acquainted with one group that vigorously opposed any membership roll. But organization is a practical necessity and a scriptural requirement.

But may not the invisible or universal church be an organism in the biological sense of a living being? Since it is clearly not a single organization, for there is no one organization that includes all Christians, must not the true church be a living being?

The answer must be No. The church cannot be a one-celled micro-organism because it clearly has many members. Now, living beings of many members, at least those of our common experience, have parents of the same species; and normally they have offspring of the same species. This is not true of the church of which Christ is the head; for there is only one head, Christ. Furthermore, this universal church had no parents and has no descendants. The church of the elect, the church that included and still includes Adam, Abraham, Moses, and Paul, is a single church. This universal church is not a genus, of which there are subspecies and particular individuals. There is only one body because there is only one head. Nor is Christ the head in any literal sense. He is not the ears or nose of the church. Nor its optic chiasm. Such materialistic views should have no place in a Christian consciousness.

The next phrase is, "who is the princeps," the beginning, the originator, the first cause, or ruler. The word was used in the plural, two verses back: thrones, lordships, *rulers*. One asks, ruler or beginning of what? No genitive follows. Some wish to connect it closely with the next four words: the beginning, that is to say, the first begotten of the dead. This would restrict the word *princeps* or *beginning* (*archē*) to the resurrection. Nothing in Greek grammar prevents such an interpretation. The second phrase could quite possibly be in apposition to the noun.

On the other hand this would make a harsh transition from the first half of the verse. The passage goes more smoothly if we say, Christ was the Creator of the world, he is the head of the church, the originator of both, the first begotten of the dead. One reason for not connecting *archē* with the resurrection of the dead, is that if *first begotten* is in apposition to *archē*, the result would be that Christ is the originator, ruler, or principle of the dead. This is too queer to accept.

The next phrase, "in order that he may have first place in everything," presents two or three difficulties. So as not to break the continuity of this somewhat lengthy explanation, it seems best to begin with the easier question of the meaning of the phrase "in all things." Since the single Greek word *all* can be masculine as well as neuter, one might propose the translation, "that he may be first among all people." Surely it cannot mean simply that Christ has first place among all the dead. That would be tautological. Of course, if

Christ rose first, he has first place. That is not worth saying. And this is another reason for refusing to restrict the word *beginning* (prince, original, or ruler), in the first half of this verse, to Christ's position among the dead. Of course, the word *first place* or *pre-eminence* could still refer to all people. But the context has spoken of the dead, of the church, and of the creation of the universe. Therefore it is better to take *all* as neuter, and ascribe pre-eminence to Christ "in every respect."

The second difficulty in verse 18 divides into several parts. First, one must ask whether the final clause is a purpose clause or a result clause. The conjunction *ina* was originally purposive; but in Koine it is often result. Which is it here?

Let us first see what reason could justify our taking it as a result clause. One might argue that the intention or purpose of our Lord in being the head of the church, and even in rising from the dead, was to redeem his elect and glorify his Father. His purpose was not to obtain any pre-eminence for himself. Yet his success in accomplishing his purpose resulted automatically in his achieving pre-eminence in every respect. Thus the clause is a result clause.

Meyer on the other hand takes it as a purpose clause: Christ is the princeps, the first begotten of the dead, in order that he may become pre-eminent. The pre-eminence is future and thus purposive. Meyer explicitly refuses to take the subjunctive verb as a present: "that he may now be pre-eminent." He also rejects the weak subjective meaning, "that he may be held to be pre-eminent." Meyer regards the subjunctive clause as strongly future. His idea is that the Messiah will become pre-eminent at the parousia. The verb itself is aorist.

The question of interpretation thus divides into two. Is the clause purposive, and if so, does it refer to the future only or to the continuing present?

Before choosing between these two interpretations, one should ask, What is the antecedent of the clause? This question is especially necessary if any purposive interpretation is to be defended. It is necessary also if one is to discard Meyer's notion of a future pre-eminence in favor of an eternal pre-eminence. Meyer wants to restrict the antecedent to the idea of the resurrection, or at most to resurrection plus headship of the church. John Eadie argues for a more inclusive antecedent. Christ's pre-eminence, even in the church, not to mention the universe, cannot depend on his resurrection alone.

In favor of identifying the antecedent as everything from verse 15 on, is the repetition of *he himself, who, by him, through him,* and *to him.* No one can fail to notice the constantly mounting emphasis on the person and role of Christt. It therefore seems arbitrary to restrict the antecedent of the purpose clause to his resurrection alone.

Incidentally, and to retrace our steps a bit, interpreting this clause as a result clause also depends on restricting the antecedent to being the head of the church. One could hardly say that Christ was the image of God, created the universe, and was before all things with the accidental result of being in first place. Therefore it is better, much better, to take the clause as purposive.

What, then, is the purpose? Meyer is quite right in rejecting the weak subjective sense that many people will come to regard Christ as pre-eminent. The sense must be objective. But the correct objective significance militates against Meyer's main contentions. Christ does not achieve pre-eminence by means of the resurrection and other events yet future. Such future events could only cause more people subjectively to recognize the position Christ already has objectively. Christ does not become pre-eminent: he is pre-eminent.

Meyer, however, insists that the verb is *become,* not *is.* To quote him verbatim: "*gignesthai* and *einai* are *never* [ital. his] synonymous." Now, certainly *gignomai* regularly means to become or come into being. Plato unequivocally separates the things that become from the realities or things that are. Being and becoming are distinct spheres.

Nevertheless, however frequent this usage is—and the lexicons give columns of references—Arndt and Gingrich give us a second meaning in Koine, "ii As a substitute for the forms of *eimi.*" Matthew 10:16 does not really mean, "Eventually become wise as serpents"; it is a present imperative, "Be wise as serpents." Mark 9:50 has the exact form that the present verse has—the subjunctive present. One could doggedly insist that Mark says, "if the salt has become unsalted"; but surely the meaning is, "if the salt be unsalted." If, however, a speck of crabbed doubt remains on Mark 9:50, Luke 1:2, written in good literary style, hardly has a speck. Luke says the early disciples were eyewitnesses from the beginning. A reader would be puzzled if Luke said the disciples *became* eyewitnesses from the beginning. Then in Luke 6:36 Christ says, "Be merciful"; he cannot have meant, "Become merciful at some future date." There are other references also.

The conclusion therefore is, not that Christ has achieved a certain degree of pre-eminence now and will later become pre-eminent in all respects, much less that he has no pre-eminence now but will later achieve it, but that he holds first place in all respects now.

1:19.   ... because [God] pleased that all the pleroma should dwell in him...

The subject of the verb *pleased* is not in the text. An English speaking person is likely to supply the word *God* in the dative: it pleased God that.... But the analogy of I Corinthians 1:21 strongly indicates that the noun *God* should be nominative: God pleased that the whole pleroma should dwell in him.

This verse, short as it is, gives the reason for Christ's pre-eminence. The reason is not Christ's resurrection. This verse gives another reason that supports the interpretation proposed for the previous verse. The reason Christ is (not will become) pre-eminent is that God pleased to have the whole pleroma dwell in him.

The meaning of *pleroma* and its relation to Gnosticism will become clearer in the next chapter. There the term is better specified as the fulness of the Godhead. Although Meyer makes a telling point that the fulness of the Godhead cannot be the meaning here because Christ's Godhead is not the result of the Father's choice or good-pleasure, but is inherently essential to Christ's person, it is hard to see what else it could mean. Certainly those commentators, both ancient and modern, are mistaken who take *pleroma* to mean the church. It is also arbitrary to interpret it as "the fulness of grace," or some other limited characteristic, when the text says *all* the fulness, the whole pleroma. Meyer is quite right to maintain that Christ's deity is not some voluntary addition that the Father conferred on the Son. Christ is God in his own right, equal to the Father in power and glory. However, this does not suffice for the weakening of the term *pleroma*. There are two reasons. First, it surely pleases the Father that the Son is the Second Person of the Trinity. Meyer talks as if anything that pleases God has to be external to him. He cannot be pleased with himself. Second, of course, God pleases to produce effects external to the Godhead. One of these external events was the incarnation and subsequent redemption. Now these both are mentioned in this same sentence, although our versification places them in the next verse. In this light it would be hard to find a word better than *eudokēsen* to cover its double object: Christ's containing the pleroma and his work of redemption.

> **1:20.** ... **and through him to reconcile the universe to himself, having made peace by the blood of his cross, by him, whether things on earth or things in heaven.**

The subject of the verb continues to be *God* (understood) in verse 19. This causes no surprise; but a careless reader might think that the next verb has Christ as subject. Was it not Christ who made peace through the blood of the cross? However, this is grammatically impossible. It is God who pleased to reconcile the universe, and it is God who made peace. Such is the syntax. But of course God made peace by the blood of Christ's cross. The *his* in "his cross" must refer to Christ.

Now, when we pause to consider, this is staggering. The preceding verses have described Christ in transcendent terms. He was the Creator, in whom all fulness dwells, the heir of the universe, for whom indeed it was created. When now the Creator of heaven and earth, the Creator himself, voluntarily suffered on the cross for our sins, we can only stand in awe and worship.

The next question is, Who reconciled whom? Of course the text says that God reconciled the world. But there is a twist in the

English usage, and we ask again, To whom was who reconciled? Were sinners reconciled to God, or God to sinners? This is not an absurd question, as if it made no difference. In human affairs there are two possibilities. Two men might commit some offense, each against the other. Both would be justifiably angry. They might later settle their difficulties. However, this case cannot illustrate the situation between God and sinners because God alone has been wronged. More nearly similar to the case of God and sinners is that in which one man has defrauded another, blackened his reputation, and violated his rights. In this case only the second man can be justifiably angry. How then may these two be reconciled? It is true that we speak of them as being reconciled to each other. But this reciprocal expression ignores the fact that one was the sinner and the other was sinned against. It is the latter who strictly must be reconciled, appeased, or propitiated. He alone has been angry and it is his anger that must be turned aside.

Hence when this verse says that God reconciled the world to himself, we see that God really reconciled himself to the world by making peace through the blood of Christ's cross. The human criminal who injures his neighbor is presumably capable of making restitution of some kind and of gaining the man's friendship again. But the religious situation is such that the offender can do nothing. It is the offended who must make peace. Now, this may not be the complete doctrine of the atonement; but it is an indispensable part of it.

That reconciliation includes sinners is no surprise to anyone who knows the least bit about the Bible; but the verse itself extends the scope of reconciliation still farther. God reconciles himself to all things—to the whole universe. Surely *ta panta* in this verse is as extensive as it was in verses 16 and 17. To this agrees the phrase "in heaven and on earth," with the particularizations of visible, invisible, thrones, and so on. Even if these particulars mainly suggest spiritual beings, the visibles would include not only human bodies but also the physical universe. While Romans 8:22 may refer only to living creatures—though *groaneth* can be taken metaphorically of mountains and stars—II Peter 3:10 more clearly indicates some purpose of God for the physical universe. This is a point only dimly apprehended by most Christians and almost completely unknown by others.

B.A.G. Fuller, an otherwise competent scholar, misunderstands Christianity, misinforms his students, and constructs an objection based on such deficiency. His aim is to show that the scope of the Bible's message is unacceptably narrow from a philosophic point of view. In his *History of Greek Philosophy* he wrote,

> The world for which the blood of redemption was spilled is the moral world. No drop of that blood overflows into the outer and physical world. In the benefits of salvation, no being, animate or inanimate, save the human, shares. The physical world remains unchanged. But after all, from the Christian point of view, why should nature be affected by the process of redemption?

Yet Christians may dimly recollect that Genesis 3:17–18 records the curse put upon the ground. And if Christians ever sing Christmas carols, they may remember,

> No more let sins and sorrows grow,
> No thorns infest the ground;
> He comes to make his blessings flow
> Far as the curse is found.

While this inclusion of the physical universe is sufficiently broad to satisfy philosophic generality, there remain a few details with respect to rational beings. It is impossible, as we have now seen, to restrict this verse to the human race, though some commentators have tried to. All the worse is a restriction to the souls of departed Christians; and utterly perverse to limit it, with Schleiermacher, to earthly and ecclesiastical relationships. It is less implausible to find in this verse a suggestion of universal salvation. Indeed, it might be so taken, were it not for the clear teaching of other New Testament passages.

A more puzzling question is: If God reconciles all things to himself, through Christ's sacrifice, and if *all* includes the righteous angels who never fell, what sort of reconciliation can they need? The ground has thorns; but the righteous angels seem to have no defects at all. Perhaps the best that can be said is that these angels rejoice at the reconciliation of sinners and come to know better what in I Peter 1:12 they could only desire to look into. This of course is supposition and not exegesis.

However some of these difficulties are resolved, it might be permissible to stretch the meaning of reconciliation beyond that of two persons re-establishing a broken friendship. Regenerated minds are so centered on the reconciliation of sinners that other facets of God's great redemptive plan escape attention. Therefore, even though some commentators oppose it, we might consider reconciliation here to be the equivalent of the word in Ephesians 1:10, translated "gather together" or better, "head up all things in Christ." The words "on earth and in heaven" occur in Ephesians as they here occur a second time to end the verse. In support of this extension of meaning, one can cite I Corinthians 15:24, 28, where it says that Christ, after all things shall have been subdued to him, will deliver up the kingdom to God, the Father, that God may be all in all.

However, this takes us too far away from the exegesis of Colossians.

> **1:21,22.** And you, who were once alienated and enemies in your minds by wicked works, he has now reconciled by the body of his flesh through death, to present you holy, unblameable, and unreproveable before him . . .

There is a textual problem here. Since the *you* at the beginning of the verse is accusative, and in conformity with the subject of the verbs in verses 19 and 20, it makes easier grammar to take the verb here as third person singular, aorist active. This makes it read, "God reconciled you." But some MSS, and the Aland text, have the second person plural, second aorist passive. This means, "you were reconciled." But although Bruce Metzger defends this reading, it reduces the sentence to nonsense. The word *you* is accusative and can be neither the subject nor the object of a passive verb. Some commentators try to escape this impasse by putting the first half of verse 22 in parentheses. But this leaves the *you* dangling. It cannot be transplanted into the parenthesis; and also with the verb inside the parenthesis the sentence is not a sentence, for it would have no finite verb. See the appendix for further information.

This verse begins a new paragraph. The preceding, instead of being regarded as reflecting the intrusion of some alien religion in Colosse, can best be taken as straightforward, dogmatic theology. It speaks of the nature, person, and position of Christ in general. There is no reason for doubting that Paul could or would write as an informative teacher. Christians often are, and ought more often to be, interested in the nature of Christ. Nevertheless at this point Paul gradually shifts from the more strictly theological exposition and returns to the theme of the early part of the chapter, namely his interest in the Colossians themselves. The transition is very smooth because the general reference to reconciliation naturally leads to the particular reconciliation of Paul's addressees.

These people were previously alienated from God. The Pharisees too were alienated from God. But the wording here resembles Ephesians 2:12 and hence may indicate that the Colossian church was at least mainly Gentile. These people were not only aliens; they were enemies. They were not only objects of divine enmity—this is obviously true—but they were actively enemies in their thinking. Romans 5:10 may also indicate this, but Romans 1:18, 21, 25 make it clearer. Their thinking was wrong. In the present century neo-orthodoxy, following Kierkegaard, and the temptation to pietism recurrent throughout church history, have led to an underevaluation of thinking. Religion, both false and true, is described as an emotion. Kierkegaard says "passion." But both Old and New Testaments emphasize thinking. They condemn a reprobate mind (Rom. 1:28, *epignōsei ... adikimon noun*), and recommend the mind of Christ (I Cor. 2:16; *nous*, mind or intellect—a good Platonic and Neoplatonic term!).

This emphasis on the intellect does not imply that external actions, whether bad or good, are of no importance. The mind controls the will. As a man thinketh, so is he. Out of the heart—the understanding—are the issues of life. In the present verse the previous enmity in the Colossians' thinking led to evil works. Luther's enemy Erasmus diluted the verse by saying, "enemies, to what? To the mind, for he who serves the flesh opposes reason." Erasmus missed the point. He views our sinful tendencies as the force of the flesh overpowering the resistance of the mind. The mind, apparently untouched by sin, lacks strength to resist the flesh. Then Erasmus translates this to mean that the sinner opposes reason. This last statement may well be true. If *reason* denotes correct thinking, surely this is in opposition to sin. But the *mind* does not always designate correct thinking. It normally refers to all thinking, good and bad. The bad thoughts of the unregenerate lead to overt evil actions. Nor is it clear what Erasmus means by the flesh. If he means gluttony and licentiousness, he is not using the term in its biblical sense. In particular this sense is quite out of accord with Paul's concern for the Colossians, for their temptation was not licentiousness but its opposite, asceticism, as we shall later see in 2:20–23. It is true, of course, that adultery and lasciviousness are works of the flesh; but so are idolatry, hatred, and excessive ambition, as Galatians 5:19–21 says. Even asceticism is a form of zeal, and hence a work of the flesh; but probably Erasmus did not have asceticism in mind.

But whether it be the asceticism at Colosse or the licentiousness in Corinth, these external actions result from thinking. Good works also result from thinking. And the contemporary irrational religion of emotion results from thinking that thinking is irreligious.

Continuing the sentence, the next verse indicates how God effected the reconciliation: "by the body of his flesh through death."

Another word of caution. Although the heresy of Docetism was to appear—the heresy that the Son of God did not have a body—it is not necessary to suppose that the Colossians were Docetic. Even their exaggerated opinion of angels does not imply such a view. The present verse is sufficiently grounded in the historical event of Jesus' death on the cross. The blood of the cross was mentioned in verse 20. This was and is an essential part of Christianity. Nothing else is needed to justify Paul's stating it.

In interpreting Scripture one's ideal is to draw out all possible implications. Possible here means valid. If one could infer from these verses the doctrine of the vicarious atonement, or even the ignominy of a crucifixion, it would be well and good. But we should ever be alert to reject invalid inferences. Ignominy and propitiation are clearly taught elsewhere; but even the inspired apostle Paul cannot condense all his teachings into a single verse. The explicit point is that reconciliation came through a bodily death.

1:22 b.   ... to present you holy and blameless and irreproachable before himself...

Here Paul states the purpose of reconciliation, or a purpose. It is futile to try to maintain that the infinitive expresses result but not purpose. Furthermore, the infinitive must depend on a finite verb; therefore, as was previously argued, the verb *reconcile* cannot be enclosed in a parenthesis.

It is God's purpose to present us holy before himself. If the grammar and the context allowed it, we would find it easier to say, Christ reconciled us in order to present us before his Father. The trouble lies in the several third person pronouns scattered through these verses. But it is rather clear that God does the reconciling, and he reconciles himself to us. The word *himself*, however, is not and should not be reflexive. Similarly the second *auton* (him) also is not reflexive: it does not have to be, it cannot be, in order to refer to God. Admittedly the language is somewhat awkward; but other interpretations are worse.

The words in between—*holy, blameless, irreproachable*—are as simple as the preceding was awkward. *Blameless* and *irreproachable* are as synonymous as any two words can be; and *holy* in this context has the same meaning. Those commentators who try to distinguish three different references in them only display their own ingenuity.

1:23.   ... if, that is to say, you remain in the faith, founded and seated and not moved away from the hope of the gospel which you heard, which was preached in all creation under heaven, of which I Paul am a deacon.

The First Chapter of Colossians

The continuous line of thought is: God reconciled himself to you by Christ's death to present you holy before himself, if indeed you remain in the faith.

It seems better to connect this last phrase with the nearer verb "to present you," rather than with the more remote verb "reconciled." But this is a matter of mere grammar and does not alter the sense. A single purpose runs through both verbs.

The *if* clause that begins the verse is variously translated. The King James entirely omits the particle *ge* and says simply "if ye continue." The New American Standard has "if indeed." The Revised Standard Version has "provided that." The Roman Catholic Jerusalem Bible puts it "as long as you persevere." Whether this last suggests more doubt than the former, one must judge for oneself. The Greek words do not suggest any serious doubt; rather *ei ge* emphasizes a condition without any suggestion that the condition will not be satisfied. We must be founded, sealed, and immovable in the faith. A person who has once confessed Jesus as Lord, and says he believes in his heart that God raised him from the dead, and then later denies the lordship of Christ and his resurrection, very probably never really believed these propositions in the first place. The person may not even have been a hypocrite. Some people's minds are wonderfully confused. The present writer knew a seminary professor who willingly and publicly subscribed to the proposition, "Jesus is Lord," but asserted with equal, or more, vigor, "I do not believe anything just because Jesus said so."

The next phrase, about the hope of the gospel, is similar to verse 5 above, to which the reader may wish to refer once again.

Following this is the puzzling statement that the gospel has been preached to every creature, if such must be the translation. But obviously the gospel has not even yet been preached to every human being. One commentator avoids the problem by calling the words a hyperbole, and refers to verse 6. But verse 6 simply says that the gospel is in the world as a whole and produces fruit wherever it is heard. In verse 15 the same phrase means the whole universe, rather than every human being. Now, further, the present verse does not say that the gospel was preached *to* every person; the words are "preached *in* all creation." Someone might wish to question this interpretation on the ground that the following words are "under heaven," and thus find favor for "every human being." This may sound plausible at first. However there are two objections. The first objection still stands, that the gospel had not been preached to every human being. The second questions the validity of the opposing argument. The argument is unclear, but it might mean that "under heaven" takes care of the fact that the gospel was not preached to the angels in heaven; therefore it must have been preached to every human being under heaven. This is clearly invalid. That the gospel was preached to no angels does not imply that it was preached to every human being. Hence it remains possible to say that the gospel was preached in the world under heaven. And this is factually true.

Finally Paul concludes, "of which I Paul became a deacon." The Greek word is *deacon*. In the present social and ecclesiastical situation it is worthwhile to note that Paul applies this word to himself. The word originally had a very wide sense. Anyone who *served* was a *deacon* (a servant). Hence Phoebe in Romans 16:1 was a "deacon." But it does not follow that she was ordained to any office. Every active church member was a deacon, a servant of the Lord. Now, it may be possible to argue that the seven deacons of Acts 6:1 ff. were never ordained—though Acts 6:6 indicates the contrary—but there is not the slightest ground in the New Testament for ordaining women to any office. The word has two distinct senses, one original, one technical. Here, where Paul could have used "apostle," he chose "servant." Could this word justify ordaining women as apostles?

> **1:24.   Now I rejoice in my sufferings for you and I fill up the deficiencies of the suffering of Christ in my flesh on behalf of his body, which is the church...**

Before the main difficulty of the verse is considered, a minor remark on its first word can be gotten out of the way. The first word is *Now*; and although there is not even the weak adversative *de* after it, it forms a contrast with the time prior to "I became a servant."

His persecuting zeal before and his present sufferings for Christ are different. The connection between verses 23 and 24 is close enough, but still verses 24–29 can be taken as a new paragraph because the interest shifts from the spiritual standing of the Colossians to the ministry of the apostle.

What then was his ministry? Were Christ's sufferings insufficient to save us? Was it necessary for Paul to suffer vicariously for the church and remedy Christ's defective sacrifice? The prepositions *ant-ana* strongly suggest substitutionary suffering; and even *uper* sometimes designates substitution. The Romanists would be very happy with such an interpretation. It would justify their doctrine of the treasury of the saints, and perhaps purgatory also. At least this verse was used by Bellarmine, Cajetan, Suarez and others to defend indulgences.

If, instead of this, the prefix *anti* indicates a substitute for Christ's sufferings, so as to make Paul a substitute for Christ instead of being a substitute for the church's penalty, the result is all the worse. But the commentator who suggested this incredibly bizarre notion cannot possibly accommodate the phrase "for . . . the church." This point will be considered more soberly a few paragraphs below.

Surprisingly Meyer in four and a half pages of dense print on this verse never mentions Romanism. This is not to say that he agrees with their apostasy. On the contrary he paraphrases the verse as "I am in the course of furnishing the complete fulfillment of what in my case still remains in arrears of fellowship of affliction with Christ." There is no mistaking Meyer's own opinion. On the next page (p. 255) he adds,

> Every explanation which involves the idea of the suffering endured by Christ in the days of his flesh having been incomplete and needing supplement, is an anomaly which offends against the analogy of faith of the New Testament.

Although this sounds good at first, there is a necessary correction that must be made a bit later.

How then can Paul fill up the deficiencies of Christ's sufferings? In opposing Romish interpretations one should not ignore the opposite extreme. Schleiermacher conjoins the tribulations of Christ with the sufferings of Paul on the ground that they were similar in nature. That they were both physical, and that they were both mental, is obviously true. Were they both vicarious? Could Paul have said, "My God, my God, why hast thou forsaken me?"

C.F.D. Moule comes closer to the truth (as the present writer sees it) except that he tries to combine two historical modes of interpretation, the first of which is still too close to Romanism. First, "Christ's sufferings (on the cross and throughout his ministry) are necessarily shared by Christians. . . . The continuance and ultimate completion of these sufferings being a part of the privilege of incorporation in the Body of Christ, is something which the apostle welcomes."

The words "on the cross" make this view unacceptable; though if they are omitted the remainder is not bad.

The second type of interpretation, the one Moule on the whole prefers, is: "There is a 'quota' of sufferings which the 'corporate Christ,' the Messianic community, the Church, is destined to undergo before the purposes of God are complete. . . ." Moule recognized here a predestinarian presupposition: "the idea of a predetermined quota of persons to be converted . . . also . . . a quota of wickedness to be completed: Matthew 23:32, I Thessalonians 2:16." Moule dislikes this predestinarian theme, but would like to retain the interpretation by submerging it. He also pays attention to the substitutionary prepositions: "the *anti* is only redundant repetition of the *uper*," and the meaning is "on behalf of."

John Eadie probably would not have disagreed with Moule on the main point, but his explanation is fuller. It is the view supported by Chrysostom, Augustine, Anselm, Luther, Calvin, Zanchius—an enormously distinguished list. This view holds that Paul's sufferings are afflictions of Christ because Christ really endured them: "he really felt them." One of these commentators used the verse, "Saul, Saul, why persecutest thou me." Thus Christ identified himself with the church and "felt" the pain of Saul's victims. So also Christ felt Paul's pain when Paul after his conversion was himself persecuted. But the language is metaphorical, for we cannot assert that God feels pain in heaven.

The First Chapter of Colossians

Now it is time to gather the acceptable ideas together. With Moule we may try to reduce *anti* to *uper* and rid ourselves of the embarrassment of Paul's making a vicarious sacrifice to complete Christ's propitiation of the Father. Perhaps one can improve slightly on Moule by noting that the *anti* here is not an independent preposition, but a prefix; and further that it is also modified by the second prefix *ana*.

Paul therefore did not suffer vicariously in propitiating the Father for the sins of the elect. Christ's vicarious sufferings were complete, adequate, and indefectible. More was neither needed nor possible. Paul suffered, not instead of the church, but on behalf of the church, enduring the persecution entailed by preaching the gospel.

There is another point. A few paragraphs back exception was taken to the phrase "on the cross" as used by Moule. There is indeed a sense in which Christ's sufferings are "shared" by Christians. We are, shall I say, disturbed by the realization that Christ had to suffer agony for us. References are found in I Peter 4:13, Matthew 20:23, and Hebrews 13:13, where Christians are "partakers" of Christ's sufferings (partaker—to have in common), or where they drink the same cup and are baptized with the same baptism, or even the milder "bearing his reproach." But in no way do our tribulations fill up or add to Christ's propitiatory merits. We do, however, suffer on behalf of the church, and in this sense complete the sufferings Christ left uncompleted.

The point of the passage, however, is not that we share in Christ's sufferings, but that our sufferings are his. As Alford again so well remarks, "All the tribulations of Christ's body are Christ's tribulations . . . and the tribulations of Christ will not be complete till the last pang shall have passed."

Thus we can accept Moule's notion, without his inconsistent distaste for its presuppositions, that there is a predestined amount of suffering yet to be endured before the culmination. In this way we can gladly "hasten" the return of our Lord.

> 1:25. . . . of which I became a deacon according to God's administration given to me toward you [your benefit] to fill up the word of God . . .

The First Chapter of Colossians

Once again, before changing the subject matter, we can observe that the idea of God's administration of the historical development ties in with the predestinarian note in the preceding verse. That Paul's ministry was a matter of predestination is clearly evident from the asserted fact that it was according to God's economy, dispensation, or administration, that Paul became a servant and enjoyed even his hardships. The repetition of the term *diakonos* contrasts with "princes of the Church," whose feet or ring the faithful must kiss (cf. Matt. 20:25).

God did, however, give Paul a dispensation or administration. What was Paul then to dispense or administer? Of what was he a steward? How in particular was he to serve? The King James Version gives an easy answer: "to fulfill the word of God." Well, no doubt Paul was going to fulfill some Old Testament prophecies. The Revised Standard Version translates it, "to make the word of God fully known," a good idea perhaps but not a good translation. Luther's Bible says, "*dass ich das Wort Gottes reichlich predigen soll*," "that I should richly preach the word of God." Ostervald in French has the same thing. The words "to you" perhaps indicate a rich preaching of the word, rather than a fulfilling of prophecy. One does not quite speak of fulfilling prophecies to someone. Ministers certainly preach to people. But there may be something more here also. To fill up the word of God may mean to complete the divine revelation. Protestants claim that the canon was closed or completed with the death of the apostles. Since then God has revealed nothing. Thus Paul is conscious that he is to fill up the word of God. Should anyone say that John lived longer than Paul and wrote after him, so that Paul did not complete the word of God, we may reply, first, that the dates of John's Gospel and the Revelation may be much earlier than early twentieth century suppositions put them; but second, and more likely, Paul regards this completion as a part of the apostolic office, so that his statement here refers not only to himself, but to the other apostles also.

With this in mind it is clear that Paul considers his epistles as the word of God, its last chapter, so to speak. In the late twentieth century it has now become popular to speak of Paul's writings as "culturally conditioned," and therefore not applicable to us today, at least in this or that regard. To decide which, if any, of Paul's sentences are not culturally conditioned, and therefore useful for the church now, it is necessary to frame criteria on the basis of this century's wisdom. Hence instead of the principle of *Sola Scriptura*, and by saving faith believing "to be true whatsoever is revealed in the Word, for the authority of God himself speaking therein" (Westminster Confession, XIV, ii), these people use their own authority and sit in judgment over the word of God.

> 1:26. ... the secret hidden from the ages and from the races, but now has been made manifest to his saints...

First, the English word *mystery*, which is the usual translation, is in this day misleading. Its present connotation is something spooky, mysterious, unintelligible, or even irrational. The actual meaning is a *secret*. One of the "mysteries" of the Pythagorean mystery religion was the prohibition of eating beans. Another was not to sit with the left leg crossed over the right. Or was it the reverse? Paul's *secret* in I Corinthians 15:51 was that not everybody will die. Many people believe it to be false, but there is nothing unintelligible about it. Here Paul speaks of something that was kept secret in previous ages, but is now revealed to first-century Christians.

Yet this language is not altogether accurate. Some Bible teachers have assumed that the secret was the Gentile's inclusion among the people of God. They then conclude, in opposition to many Old Testament passages, that there was no prophecy predicting such inclusion. In fact the Scofield Bible held that not even the death of Christ was predicted, for, to summarize his words, the next event in the order of prophecy as it then (at Christ's birth) stood was the restoration of the Jewish kingdom (note on Matthew 4:17).

The more accurate paraphrase of the verse is: the inclusion of the Gentiles—not the prediction, but the event—was hidden, but is now fulfilled before the eyes of the saints. The statement in Ephesians 3:5 is fuller: The secret was not made known to other generations *as it* has *now* been revealed.

1:27. ... [to his saints] to whom God willed to make
known what the wealth of the glory of this mystery
among the Gentiles [is], which is Christ in you, the hope
of glory...

Herbert M. Carson (*in loc.*) is willing to speak of "God's eternal
purpose," as the meaning of the first verb. Eadie not only is silent
on predestination but even wants to delete any suggestion of free
grace. He reduces the phrase to the idea that God merely desired to
give the saints more information—which of course God did. But the
good pleasure of God is more than that.

God chose to make known how great the glory of this mystery is.
Perhaps some expositors are right in saying that the use of nouns
instead of adjectives makes the verse more majestic. It is certainly
emphasis by repetition.

Although many eminent theologians in the Reformation century
interpreted the mystery to be the gospel itself, there are two reasons to think otherwise. First, God preached the gospel beforehand
to Abraham; but of course not as it has now been manifested. However, and more conclusively, the secret is here explicitly connected
with the Gentiles. This allows us to refer to the far more detailed
account through chapters two and three of Ephesians. There it explains that the Gentiles, who had been aliens from the common-
wealth of Israel, have become the Israel of God. The rich glorious
secret, now realized, is "Christ in you [the Colossians], the hope of
glory."

There is a question as to the antecedent of the relative pronoun
which. It could refer to the mystery: both are neuter, and *mystery* is
the nearest possible noun. It could also refer back to *the wealth* of
the glory of the mystery, for *wealth* is also neuter. Eadie believes
that the former

> ... "yields but a bold interpretation; for it is not the fact that
> Christ was among the Gentiles, but the character and relations
> of that fact that the apostle dwells on. Nor is the antecedent
> merely *ploutos* [wealth] ... nor simply *doxa* [this is impossible
> because *doxa* is feminine] ... for the reference is not to the

The First Chapter of Colossians

> riches of the glory by themselves, but to those riches possessed
> and enjoyed by the Gentile converts."

Some people may find this acceptable; others will not be convinced. It is not a matter of Greek grammar (except for *doxa*), but of interpretation.

Well, then, either the wealth of glory or the mystery itself (the mystery itself is glorious) consists of Christ's spiritual presence among the Gentiles by the preaching of the gospel to them. And Christ's presence among them is their hope of glory. The glory which they hoped for—Christ being its foundation—presumably is the resurrection and everlasting felicity in heaven. One must emphasize Christ as the foundation of their hoping, because it is not just their subjective hoping that Paul envisages, but the objective hope, Christ himself, is their hope.

1:28. ... **whom we preach, admonishing every man and teaching every man in all wisdom, that we may present every man perfect in Christ,...**

When Paul says, "Whom we preach" he means more than the insipid statement that he has been preaching for a while. Nor is the phrase a particular claim to apostolic authority. Rather it is an emphasis on the person, nature, and work of Christ. To paraphrase it, one might say: this is the kind of Messiah-Savior-Lord I talk about. In the present century there have been and are seemingly devout persons whose slogan is, "No creed but Christ." This is far from Paul's concept. The Christology of the New Testament is admirably summed up in the Creed of Chalcedon; and those who repudiate this creed, and all creeds on principle, are simply not Christians. There may indeed be any number of people in the churches who have never heard of Chalcedon. There are undoubtedly some who have never heard of one person and two natures—a disgrace to the church they attend—but there is a great difference between being an ignorant Christian and being a witting repudiator of the doctrine. In a Methodist council 50 years ago there was a speech against

65

The First Chapter of Colossians

theological formulations, creeds, doctrines, coupled with a vigorous plea to uphold Christ. Then a pastor from Haddonfield, N.J., arose and asked, "Which Christ?" It was a most pertinent question, for there is the legendary Christ of Strauss, the ethical Christ of Renan, the insane Christ of Albert Schweitzer, and the mythological unknowable Christ of Bultmann. "Which Christ?" is always a pertinent question. It is most unfortunate if some parishioners are so ignorant as to be unable to see the difference. Our judgment of charity that these people are themselves Christians is probably often mistaken. To distinguish and thus to make the elementary steps in Christian growth, one must know the Creed of Chalcedon, if not by name and by heart—few people can recite it—most certainly by concept and intelligible content. This is he "whom we preach."

The remainder of the verse emphasizes Paul's admonitions. Note here the threefold repetition of "every man." There may be today some humble, self-effacing souls who say and even think that theology is too much for their limited mentality. I suspect there are more who find theology too much for their unlimited indolence. But Paul makes no exceptions: he admonishes every man and teaches every man in all wisdom: not merely the wisdom of Nicene and Chalcedon, but also of the Heidelberg catechism and the Westminster Confession. He was guiltless of the blood of all men because he taught the whole counsel of God. Contemporary ministers—without referring to those who reject the inerrancy of God's word—are inclined, often on purpose, to truncate the gospel, the message, the truth.

This is tragic, for it defeats Paul's purpose, which was "to present every man perfect in Christ." Of course Paul did not accomplish his purpose. The deplorable literary remains of the subapostolic authors show how little they understood the divine revelation. No doubt Paul well knew that his ideal would not be realized; but he was faithful to his ideal and God's command nevertheless.

The desirability of a full knowledge of God, rather than a mere smattering, is evidenced in the words "all wisdom." It is not that Paul in all his wisdom teaches every man something; but that Paul instructs every man in all the wisdom God has revealed. Widespread contemporary religious opinion holds wisdom and knowledge in low esteem. The tenor of the majority of evangelical churches is anti-intellectual. The faculties and chapel speakers in Christian colleges frequently warn the students not to let their academic endeavors injure their devotion. Then they hold a pep rally for the football team. Paul on the contrary contrasted the corruptible crown of the pagan Greek Olympics with the incorruptible crown of the Christian.

This latter crown is the aim of the teaching. Paul taught every man in order to present each one before God perfect in Christ.[2]

It may seem strange that Paul expresses himself in this manner. He speaks as if "we," i.e., Paul and Epaphras, are going to present their converts to God on the day of judgment. The idea of Paul's presenting these converts to God as a functionary introduces various subjects to their earthly monarch is obviously far-fetched. Paul might recommend them to God in his daily prayers. The verb *paristēmi* can mean, *present*, *place at the disposal of*, *represent*, or even *render*, as well as to *bring before a judge*. It is then Paul's purpose to make them or render them complete, perfect, mature in Christ.

Some recent theologians have made considerable use of the phrase "in Christ." It is not easy to know what sense they attach to it. There are instances where they insist that predestination must always be "in Christ," as if the Reformers thought otherwise. One not so radical commentator wrote, "The phrase 'perfect in Christ' does not simply mean perfect in knowledge . . . as Chrysostom and Calvin supposed." He then tries to describe it as "fellowship with him" and "in likeness to him." But are we not like Christ if we have the mind of Christ? There is no objection to using the phrase "like Christ"; but it is better to know in what particulars we are or will be

---

2. This commentator has tried rather deliberately to restrict himself to the text of the Colossian letter, and avoid bringing in material from other parts of the New Testament, or even from other Pauline epistles. A pure and rigid adherence to this principle, if not literally impossible, would be stupid, for the interpretation of at least some of the text requires an examination of Paul's use of words elsewhere. But clearly too much of this would lead, not so much to a commentary on Colossians, as to a theology of the New Testament. For example, how many of the following passages on teaching, doctrine, wisdom, understanding should be included here? Acts 20:20–31; Romans 1:14 (on "every man"); I Corinthians 1:30, 2:6–7, 2:16, 3:2; I Timothy 3:2; II Timothy 2:24, 4:2; Titus 1:9; Hebrews 6:1–2; plus a score of passages in the Gospel of John.

like him. Calvin did not use such vague expressions. To be mature is to have an extensive *knowledge* of Christ. Since God would not have put a means in Paul's hands insufficient to attain God's and Paul's purpose, and since the means was the preaching of Pauline theology, it follows that maturity is a knowledge and belief in those holy doctrines. That is why, again, he said, "Whom we preach." And he adds:

> **1:29.** ... to which [end] **I** also labor, straining [agonizing] in proportion to the energy with which he energizes me in power.

This translation would not be satisfactory for a version of the New Testament, but it may convey a sense of the Greek phraseology. In view of what nearly every Bible believer knows of Paul's sufferings, it is not hard to understand the verse. Perhaps the only admonition that an expositor need give is to avoid thinking that Paul's struggles were only his physical persecutions. The verb *agonidzomai* does not connote the sufferings of persecution, but very definitely the straining of an athlete to win a contest. He strained to preach and teach. And many faithful pastors and especially foreign missionaries have some appreciation of the difficulties involved.

The Second Chapter

2:1. For I want you to know how much agony I endure for you and those of Laodicea, and all who have not seen my face in the flesh...

The chapter divisions in our modern Bibles, like the verse divisions, do not exist in the Greek manuscripts. Therefore the beginning of a new chapter does not necessarily indicate a logical division of thought. A minor division could have begun at 1:29, for 1:29 and 2:1 are identical in subject matter. Then this minor division might end with 2:5, for it tells of Paul's personal straining and agonizing. But even so, these verses are a sort of parenthesis in a great Christological passage.

The first verse states a reason for something. Its reference seems to be the preceding verse: Paul explains that he mentions his struggles *because* he wants the Colossians and the Laodiceans to know how concerned he is for them, even though he has never met them. Meyer calls this interpretation "erroneous," but it is hard to see what other interpretation makes sense. Meyer tries to say that verse 1 is a specific instance that Paul uses to confirm verse 29. But there is nothing specific about it, for it does not refer to some definite event, such as his being stoned in Lystra or the riots in Ephesus. In neither of these cases did Paul suffer particularly for the Colossians or the Laodiceans. The result is that Paul mentioned his struggles generally because he wanted them to know his concern for them.

It is to be admitted that the commentators differ. The Huguenot Daillé strongly urges that Paul had previously visited Colosse, and that therefore many there had seen his face. But he also holds (in opposition to the nineteenth-century Meyer) that Paul here speaks of all throughout the empire who had not seen him, rather than simply of whoever in Colosse had missed him on that prior visit. The reader will no doubt agree with the Frenchman that the matter is of slight importance—and yet we have some interest in Paul's itineraries.

> **2:2.** ... **in order that their hearts may be confirmed, being united in love and to all the wealth of the full conviction of the understanding, to knowledge of the secret of God [i.e. ?] of Christ...**

The King James translation says, "that their hearts might be comforted." This English may have been appropriate in 1611, but in 1978 it gives the wrong sense. The Latin etymology of *comfort* goes back to the word for *strength*, as with a military *fort*. The Greek word can mean: to *summon* someone to your aid, to urge, exhort, encourage; implore or entreat; cheer up, or comfort. There is no indication that the Colossians needed cheering up: they, like us all, needed to be encouraged and strengthened. If anyone say that *hearts* need cheering up, while only *minds* and especially *wills* need strengthening, let it be remembered, first, that in Scripture it is the *heart* that does the thinking and willing; second, that Paul is teaching doctrine and refuting error; and, third, that he has just referred to straining and agonizing. A person struggling against enemies might want some cheering up, but his real need is strength. Moule suggests "stiffened to boldness." Confirmation in the truth is the appropriate idea in this passage.

The reason Paul says "their hearts" instead of "*your* hearts," is that he has just mentioned the Laodiceans and whoever has never seen his face.

In the agony of battle, union is highly desirable. One admires Athanasius *contra mundum*, and the Sunday School children sing, "Dare to be a Daniel, dare to stand alone." Excellent, and in these two and other instances, necessary. But union with others is better. Carson says it well:

> In view of the debilitating effect of false teaching upon the spiritual life... this inner strengthening was a primary need.... Error is divisive. It breaks up the unity of the body of believers. Thus the unifying power of a God-given love for Christ and for one another will be a means of resisting this spiritual corrosion from without.

In view of contemporary misuse of the concept of love, it is well also to quote Daniel, Bishop of Calcutta and Metropolitan of India (1846): "We must not confound this blessed grace of love with indifference to truth..." (*in loc.*).

The next word, *and*, introducing a purpose clause, is hard to construe. The difficulty consists in relating the verb *may be strengthened*, the participle *being united*, plus the clause *and to all wealth*. One may explain it by making the participle parenthetical: "that their hearts (being united) may be strengthened for the purpose of receiving all wealth." However, the parenthesizing of *being united* seems a bit artificial, although participles lend themselves so; and it fails to account for the following conjunction. For a second possibility one may make *united* and *to all wealth* coordinate, both dependent on the verb. This would make it: "that you may be strengthened by being united and to all wealth." The difficulty here is that of a conjunction connecting a participle and a clause which contains no verbal form at all. There is a third possibility: the non-parenthetical *united* can depend immediately on the verb, and the purpose clause can be subordinate to the participle. Yet, since a conjunction regularly connects coordinate elements, grammar does not favor it. Indeed, in this case there should be no conjunction at all. We are left therefore with the peculiar coordination of a verbal and a nonverbal clause. This seems awkward, but it also seems to be the least of the grammatical difficulties. On the other hand, the sense of the paragraph seems to be: "I want you to know my struggles that your hearts being united in love may be strengthened for the purpose of obtaining all the wealth" (next to be mentioned).

What does the wealth of a Christian consist of? Answer: It consists of the fulness of the understanding. One's full conviction of the understanding is the settled and fixed persuasion that one comprehends the truth, and that it is the truth that is comprehended. Such a one is not blown hither and yon by every wind of doctrine. A person ever learning and never able to grasp the truth is not Paul's ideal. If Paul spoke to the Colossians as he did, the Colossians being new Christians recently detached from a pagan culture, how much more do his exhortations apply to us who have profited by centuries of instruction? We have studied Athanasius, Augustine, Calvin; still some of us do not take kindly to clear cut unambiguous doctrine. Such people are poverty stricken. They have never earned the riches Paul offers. It takes earning. Faith or belief is indeed a gift from God; but one cannot believe what is revealed without studying the Bible. That is why some people write commentaries. That is why Paul says "whom we preach."

Paul emphasizes understanding and intelligence, for after writing "all the wealth of the full conviction of the intelligence," he repeats the idea in a parallel phrase, "knowledge of the secret of God, of Christ." Some commentators (e.g., Eadie, Lightfoot, et al) take *gnosis* as plain knowledge, and *epignosis* as much fuller knowledge. That Paul is intensely interested in knowledge, in full knowledge, in strong meat rather than babies' milk, is indubitable; but the point does not depend on the prepositional prefix. There is little if any discernible difference in usage. The idea of full knowledge comes with words such as *full*, *all* wisdom, *mature* or perfect, rather than with *upon* (*epi*, the prefix).

The object of the knowledge in this case is the secret of God, of Christ. Above the mystery or secret was the inclusion of the Gentiles. We today, both because today is nearly two thousand years afterward and because we are not Jews, can hardly understand the revolutionary character of bringing the Gentiles under the covenant with Abraham and Moses. True, the Jews would not have been shocked by a few or even many Gentiles becoming Jews. But a predominantly Gentile church, the abrogation of the Mosaic sacrifices, and especially the cessation of circumcision as a necessary religious rite, staggered them beyond measure. We today fail to realize how great a change this entailed. But in this verse the mystery is identified as Christ. The word *Christ* is in apposition with *mystery*, not with God. This does not amount to a contradiction or even to a modification, for the following phrase in verse 3 covers the preaching of the gospel to the Gentiles and it covers the gospel itself.

2:3. ... in whom are all the treasures of wisdom and knowledge hidden...

The word *thēsauroi* can mean either a storehouse (a treasury) or its contents. Since here the noun is plural, the idea of contents fits better.

Some commentators wish to read *in which* instead of *in whom*. The neuter receives some support from 1:26, where the *mystery* is *hidden*. But there is greater support for the masculine *in whom*, i.e., in Christ. First, the word *Christ* immediately precedes the relative phrases; second, the great Christological section places more emphasis on Christ than on the mystery; third, it is not true that all the treasures of wisdom are contained in the mystery, but rather the mystery and all other knowledge is contained in Christ.

Some of the older and more imaginative theologians try to distinguish between *wisdom* and *knowledge*. One of them makes *wisdom* refer to divine matters and *knowledge* to human affairs. Equally unfortunate is Lightfoot's explanation:

> While *gnosis* is simply *intuitive*, *sophia* is *ratiocinative* also. While *gnosis* applies chiefly to the apprehension of truths, *sophia* superadds the power of reasoning about them and tracing their relations.

The Second Chapter of Colossians

More sober, but equally wrong is to refer *wisdom* to morality and *knowledge* to science or academic philosophy. As a matter of fact, *philosophy*, during the last two centuries B.C., and the first two of our era, was mainly ethical; but this indicates the center of interest, and not the meaning of the word. Contrary to Eadie, Calvin has our approval when he fails to find much difference in meaning between the two words and explains their occurrence as literary emphasis.

Instead of so much stress being laid on the effect of Gnosticism or other Greek religions on the Colossians, it is better to note how Paul's message applies to the Jews. Although information relative to the Jewish population in Colosse is as sparse as that relating to Gnosticism, to whom, more than to the Jews, can all this be a refutation of one point of view? It was the Jews who had to be convinced that Jesus was the Messiah and that the Messiah was no mere man or even angel, but God on high.

This theme had to be drummed into the ears and minds of some three hundred bishops also in A.D. 325, and none of these was either Gnostic or Jew. This theme failed to win acceptance by Servetus and Socinus at the time of the Reformation. This theme too was the object of attack by the New England Unitarians. It is therefore a theme that should, in every time and place, be promulgated with vigor. Nevertheless, there are places and times, when, because the main doctrine is not contested, the second point of importance needs more emphasis. This second point is that Christ is the storehouse of all wisdom and knowledge. The reference here is not to pseudo-science, "scientism," or atheism, for people in this camp need the main message. The reference is to professing evangelicals. At the present time there is a recrudescence of pietism, so-called nondoctrinal Christianity, a religion of pious—supposedly pious—feelings, and anti-intellectual dependence on emotions. Since God will not permit his church and his gospel to be extinguished, such falsehood will fail and the truth will prevail. God accomplishes this through human means, and these means are faithful preachers of Paul's letter to the Colossians.

To return for a final moment to modern science, one notes that the word *all* implies that science is neither wisdom nor knowledge. Knowledge, in its objective sense of truth, never changes. Science has always been changing, with an ever increasing acceleration. Hence, there is no truth in physics and chemistry. But for more on this point, see *The Philosophy of Science*, by the present writer.

2:4.   This I say in order that no one deceive you by persuasive fallacies.

The demonstrative *this* no doubt refers to what Paul said about the treasures of wisdom and knowledge in verse three, or at most goes back to the last half of verse two. That is, Paul insists that all knowledge is in Christ in order to guard the Colossians against deception. The translation above is not strictly literal. The verb is *paralogize*, from which the English term *paralogism* is derived. This noun refers to logical fallacies. The final noun simply means persuasive speech. To avoid deception by persuasive fallacies, one ought to know a little logic, the rules of inference for example; one must avoid ambiguities by insisting on strict definition; and then one must consider the truth or falsity of the premises. False teachers misuse all three to deceive inattentive Christians.

2:5.   ... for even though I am absent in the flesh, nevertheless I am with you in spirit, rejoicing as I see your orderliness and the solidity of your faith in Christ.

Lightfoot sees in *taxin* a reference to military order, and *stereōma* becomes a solid phalanx. Of course Paul and the Colossians knew about military matters, and this could be such an allusion. The main idea, however, is Paul's serious concern for the Colossians, which concern he uses as a basis for the further exhortation.

2:6.   Accordingly, as you received the Anointed Messiah, Jesus the Lord, walk in him...

The term *Christ* long ago became a proper name. It is so used in the New Testament. But the usage was just beginning, so that it frequently retained its significance as a title. Here the term is followed by a personal identification, Jesus the Lord; and therefore it is plausible to take *Christ* in this instance as a title. One may also note in the name *Jesus* a reference to the historical person, the man who walked the roads of Galilee and Judea. Then, having identified the historical Jesus, Paul immediately applies to him the title which the Septuagint uses for JHWH. Jesus is Jehovah—though Jehovah's Witnesses do not realize it.

The Colossians had accepted or received the Christ, and on this basis Paul urges them to walk in him. Some pages back a reference was made to the words "in Christ." In this century some theologians, not alert to figures of speech, impose a mystical meaning on the phrase. They seem to take it as a literal merging of persons. In the early Middle Ages John Scotus Eriugena supposedly advocated a union of personalities such that the human Christian became God. Probably this was not what Eriugena meant; but mysticism tends in that direction. We should think more soberly and recognize figures of speech for what they are. To walk "in Christ" means to conduct oneself, to live one's life, in obedience to Christ's precepts. Possibly the difficulty in doing so produces an inclination toward mystical ease.

2:7. ... having been rooted in and being built on him, and being confirmed in the faith as you were taught, abounding in thanksgiving.

This last half of the sentence seems to have mixed metaphors—one of a plant and the other of a building. But it was not uncommon to speak of planting a city; and I Corinthians 3:9 combines agriculture and architecture. But the more peculiar mixture is between the imperative verb *walk*, the last word of verse 6, and these two participles singly or together. One cannot walk, if he is rooted to the ground. The conflict, of course, arises from a reader's trying to combine the literal with the metaphorical meaning.

Infinitely more important than mixed metaphors is the idea that Christians are rooted in or founded upon *him*, Christ. What does it mean to have *him* as our foundation? The next words give the answer. We are strengthened, established, or confirmed in the faith. The preposition *in* may perhaps be bracketed; but the noun is preceded by the definite article: "the faith." This dative case can be an instrumental dative (confirmed by the faith), or the dative of respect, essentially the same as the accusative of specification. The King James translation is equally good: "stablished in the faith." It means that the person is altogether convinced that the gospel is true.

That this phrase refers to the truth of the gospel, and not to the subjective act of believing, is made clear in the next two phrases: "as you were taught." The faith is something taught. It is information—good news. The verb *taught* shows clearly that Paul is not thinking about the subjective activity of believing, but about the doctrines believed. If we give thanks for our subjective actions, we would be glorifying ourselves. On the contrary, the Colossians and we today are to stand firm in the faith, in the divine doctrines, and give thanks that God has given us such information and has caused us to believe the message. There can be no believing without something to believe. The particular belief here referred to is the doctrine of the person and nature of the Christ, not excluding such other matters as effectual calling, justification, immediate imputation, and so on. But here the position of Christ is the doctrine emphasized.

Again this interpretation is supported by the next three words: "abounding in thanksgiving." Were we to give abounding thanks for our own act of believing, it could possibly be similar to the prayer, "I thank God I am not like other men." There is, admittedly, a sense in which such a prayer is legitimate, though the expression is awkward. But there is no hesitation as to the legitimacy of giving thanks for the good news. Insincerity, pride, and hypocrisy are not found in thanking God for his revealed teachings.

2:8. **Take care that there shall be no one who carries you away as his prey through his philosophy and empty deceit, according to the traditions of men, according to the elements of the world, and not according to Christ.**

The Second Chapter of Colossians

It is possible that in this warning Paul has in mind one particular man, of whose destructive activity Epaphras or someone has informed him. The word is singular: "he who carries you away as prey"—a participle with its article, o sulagōgōn.

This definite, or indefinite, man may succeed by his philosophy and empty deceit. Sometimes this verse is used to discourage Christians from studying philosophy. One example is a seminary president who rigidly excludes from the curriculum any course in apologetics. Whether or not he quotes Tertullian's famous phrase, "What has Athens to do with Jerusalem?" it should be noted that Tertullian advocated a philosophy; and strange to say, it was a materialistic philosophy. If Tertullian had studied more philosophy, he might have avoided materialism. In fact those Christians who know little logic and less philosophy are precisely the ones who are most apt to be deceived by persuasive fallacies. As a nontheological layman can be deceived by Jehovah's Witnesses or some other heretical theory, so a person whose mind is formed by current opinion does not know the sources of his ideas and therefore dilutes what little Bible he knows with themes from Hegelianism, Logical Positivism, or, more usually in the present decades, Existentialism. Such people caused Paul pain, and damaged their own souls. They followed, or at least they were in danger of following, of being carried away as prey by, the traditions of men.

At this point the first word of the verse demands attention: *Look out, Beware, See to it*. Paul's exhortation, indeed his command, cannot be obeyed unless one takes care to understand the enemy. In chess a fine player lays a trap for his opponent. If the latter has not studied and does not see his opponent's scheme, he will probably lose. If he has studied the openings carefully, he will not be deceived. Paul's warning is, Beware, Take care, Be Prepared; don't be caught ignorant.

To this phrase Paul adds, "according to the elements of the cosmos and not according to Christ. What did Paul mean by "the elements of the cosmos"? If this epistle were an ancient Greek treatise on nature, the word would have designated earth, air, fire, and water—the "chemical" elements of the physical world, as the Greeks usually thought of it. But Colossians is not such a treatise. In fact there is no compelling reason to think that Paul had Greek philosophy in mind at all. Persons with a slim knowledge of the Hellenistic age, and with a queer antipathy to Plato, though not to Aristotle, very frequently assume that Paul refers to Plato. Or was it Democritus? No, since the word *elements* is plural it cannot be Democritus—it must be Empedocles. These superficial readers never dream that Paul might possibly have Jewish philosophy in mind. Josephus (*Antiquities*, 18, 1, 2) writes,

> "The Jews had for a great while three sects of philosophy peculiar to themselves, the sect of the Essenes, and the sect of the Sadducees, and the third sort of opinions was that of those called Pharisees. . . ."

The point here is that Josephus called the views of these groups "philosophy." Why must Paul have used the word in its purely Greek sense, when he himself had been educated as a Pharisee? Furthermore, the word *traditions* suggests a Jewish rather than a Greek background.

Since Colossians is a religious and not a scientific production, some commentators take the term *elements* to mean cosmic spirits, or even demonic powers, who control phenomena. This interpretation gains some weak support from the "principalities and powers" of 1:16 and 2:10,15. But, first, Paul never teaches that cosmic spirits and demons control phenomena. Second, the context indicates something different. Note that the phrase "according to the elements of the cosmos,"—better, the first principles of the cosmos—is in apposition to the phrase "the tradition of men." Paul is talking about instruction, philosophy, traditions, and persuasive paralogisms. Later in the chapter, 2:20-23, he is more specific. These verses concern the "rudiments"—the same word "elements"—of the world. Verse 21 identifies one. It is a maxim or precept. Therefore it is better to understand these worldly elements as being the axioms, presuppositions, or even the main theorems of false religions. Paul doubtless had Judaism in mind, but the exhortation is completely general.

The contrast comes in theology, doctrine, beliefs, teachings, according to Christ. So once again the reader is returned to the great Christological passage in chapter one.

2:9. Because in him there dwells all the fulness of the Godhead bodily.

The contrast between the fallacious deceit of human traditions and all the treasures of wisdom and knowledge lies in the fact that in Christ there dwells all the fulness of the Godhead bodily. This verse is the only verse which might seem to indicate that Paul is directly attacking Gnosticism. In the schemes of Basilides and Valentinus, all the fulness of the Godhead, or Pleroma, was indeed contained in Christ, but not bodily. Thus the divine person did not die on the cross. However, this verse does not require a Gnostic reference, for the same is true of Docetism also; and from another point of view the Jews also rejected the proposition.

Aside from any reference to Gnosticism, the general question remains as to the force of the word *bodily*. The word *fulness* indicates the contents; for example, "The earth is the Lord's, and the fulness thereof." The fulness of the Godhead is the totality of perfections, attributes, or qualities of deity. These include self-existence, sovereignty, omnipotence, and the like. The question now is, how do these exist in Christ bodily?

The question is sharpened by the word *Godhead*. Commentators regularly contrast the word in this verse (*theotēs*) with a similar but different word (*theiotēs*) in Romans 1:20, where the King James uses the same translation: "Godhead." The latter refers to divine qualities and can be diluted to the level of such qualities as they appear in exceptionally qualified men. Or, as in Romans, the word can refer to some divine attributes while excluding others. But *theotēs* refers strictly to the full divine nature as such—to deity itself.

C.F.D. Moule acknowledges this distinction, but when the word *bodily* is added, he writes,

> Commentators . . . group themselves . . . round five interpretations: (i) 'as an organized body,' i.e., the totality of the Godhead

is 'not distributed through a hierarchy of beings'... but gathered into one 'organism' in Christ.... (ii) expressing itself through the Body [of Christ, i.e., the church].... (iii) 'actually'—in concrete reality, not in mere seeming.... (iv) 'in essence.' So the Greek Fathers and Calvin. (v) 'assuming a bodily form,' 'becoming incarnate.' Of these, (iv) seems highly improbable, if intelligible at all.

Putting it a little more strongly than does Moule, the present writer notes that the first of these four requires either a Gnostic reference or a reference to Philo. Ronald Nash thinks that the phraseology of the Epistle to the Hebrews betrays a knowledge of Philo. This is chronologically possible, since Philo died around A.D. 40 or 50. But as for Colossians Moule remarks that it depends on a single adverb, "a slender peg on which to hang so mighty a thought."

The second interpretation is so far-fetched that we shall waste no time on it.

The third and fifth together, as Moule says, "seem on the whole to present the fewest difficulties." This is certainly so: the fulness of the Godhead was *actually* and *really* there, not there in mere appearance only. And *there* is the *incarnate* Christ. But however true this is, it is vague and incomplete.

To complete (iii) and (v), number (iv) must be added. Moule dismissed it as hardly intelligible. But the Greek fathers and Calvin are not usually unintelligible. The three views are compatible and complementary. The fourth means that the *essence*, i.e., the definition, the reality of God, dwelt in the body of Jesus. Of course Jesus' body as such was not omniscient, for bodies know nothing; nor was it omnipresent, for bodies are locally restricted. But the ego, the person, whose body and instrument it was, satisfied the complete definition of deity.

Another possible interpretation, or implication, one that Moule does not mention, is the Lutheran doctrine of the *communicatio idiomatum*. This means that the characteristics of the divine nature are also common to the human nature.

But a *communicatio idiomatum* ought to work both ways. If the divine attributes are common to the physical body, the characteristics of time, space, form, and tactual qualities should be held in common by the divine essence. But this implication, that God has physical and temporal form, is hard to swallow. Perhaps the *communicatio* relates only to mental, not to physical, characteristics. In this case the thinking of the Father would be temporal, and he also would be ignorant of the date of Christ's return. At any rate, the Lutheran interest is not on Jesus' mind or soul. The *communicatio* refers to Jesus' body. And for this reason the word *bodily* in the verse under consideration serves Lutheran purposes. The reason is that their doctrine of the *communicatio idiomatum* is essential to their sacramental theory of consubstantiation. Christ's body is ubiquitous, and therefore that body is with, in, and under the bread wherever communion is celebrated. Calvinists object that first this violates the law of contradiction, and second its sacramentarianism is as unbiblical as the Romish transubstantiation.

So much for that. But before leaving the verse, the word *Godhead* needs further comment. To what was said a few paragraphs back, a remark should be made relative to the doctrine of the Trinity. American Christians in their pews—Bible believing Christians—are apt to think of the Father, the Son, and the Holy Spirit, and then stop thinking. If they are not consciously tritheists, neither do they clearly envisage the unity of the Godhead. Some who think a little more and have just a smattering of philosophic terms consider the Father as the unity, and the Son and Spirit as the diversity. Thus they attempt to solve "the One-and-the-Many problem" which Parmenides discovered and removed by denying plurality, which Democritus hardly considered at all, which embarrassed Plato, in which Plotinus failed horribly, and in which also William James turned Parmenides upside down by denying unity. The contemporary theologians may go further and constructively propose that unity and plurality are "equally ultimate" in the Godhead. They are not apt to have a very clear idea of what "equally ultimate" means.

The orthodox doctrine of the Trinity certainly teaches that the Father and the Son are equal in power and glory, and, as equally eternal, they may be called equally ultimate. But the Father is not to be equated with unity and the Son with plurality. The three persons are the plurality and the Godhead is the unity. The Godhead is not one of the persons as distinct from another, but rather the common reality shared by the three. Such is our partial answer to the objections of Islam, and also to some confused American theologians. But whether the group of common qualities, the Godhead, is more ultimate than any one of the three persons who share these attributes, and whether "ultimate" means "generic," for certainly there is no chronological precedence in this argument, are questions more properly discussed in a systematic theology than in an exegesis of Colossians.

2:10.   . . . and you have been filled by him who is the head of every principality and power;

Although the noun *plēroma* of the preceding verse carries over to the participle *peplērōmenos* here, no one can suppose that human beings contain or are filled with all the fulness of the Godhead. We reject all mystical merging of persons. Every man is an island. He is not somebody else. He surely is not God. The three persons of the Trinity and the billions of human persons remain, each one, indefeasibly self-identical forever.

The verse says that we have been filled by Christ, not with Christ. The Father does not pour Christ into our bodies as one might fill a glass by pouring water from a large pitcher. In another respect also the metaphor of the glass is poor. A glass always has the same cubic content. A person's mind, we hope, increases. So Christ pours more into the middle-aged than into the less-aged. If we have been filled full at the moment, we are encouraged by knowing that we shall later expand and understand more.

No doubt we are filled with, or, better, from the fulness of the Godhead—filled with the treasures of wisdom and knowledge. But the emphasis falls on him who fills us out of his storehouse of treasure. We have been filled by Christ. Augustine and Calvin did not fill us, though God surely used them as means. The analogy of the glass, like all analogies, is further defective. When a glass is filled, it does nothing itself. But our filling requires some activity on our part. We must read the Bible, pay attention to a sermon, follow the tedious intricacies of this commentary, and meditate day and night. No doubt God causes us to do these things; nevertheless and therefore it is we who do them. The verb here is not imperative. The verse is declarative: you have been filled. But even to receive information, it is necessary to pay attention.

The final phrase of the verse is, "who is the head of every principality and power." Thus the Christological theme continues. The phrase itself is a repetition of the items in verse 16 of the first chapter. Later also there will be another reference to these powers. Paul warns us not to worship them.

> **2:11,12.** . . . by whom also you were circumcised with a circumcision made without hands, in the stripping off of the body of flesh, by the circumcision of Christ, being buried with him in baptism, with whom also you have been raised through faith in the power of God who raised him from the dead.

These two verses present several difficulties. Some degree of attention is required. First, contrary to one commentator who thinks that baptism is the means by which God fills us, the verse does not describe any method "how this 'completeness' which has been brought within human range by the incarnation, is appropriated." Such an interpretation is ruled out on the ground that the verse is introduced by the conjunction *and*, not by the conjunction *for*. The translation, therefore, is "and by whom" or "by whom also." Thus these two verses are something additional. Besides the word *also*, the sense itself shows that it cannot refer to the completeness of the earlier verse; for neither baptism, nor the inclusion in the covenant of which it is a sign, nor even regeneration, puts into our minds the understanding, wisdom, and knowledge that constitute that fulness.

Paul now seems to say that baptism is a circumcision, made without hands, that displaces Jewish circumcision. At first this seems peculiar, for baptism is performed by the hands of a minister as truly as circumcision is performed by the hands of a priest. Well, then, perhaps this is not exactly the comparison Paul has in mind.

To clear up this puzzle one must note some Old Testament material on circumcision. This is necessary because sacramentarians tend to evaluate circumcision lower than is right in order to evaluate baptism more highly than it should be.

First of all, circumcision was not initiated by the Mosaic law. God gave the sign of his covenant to Abraham. The sign of course was administered by the hands of men, and to children, some of whom were never regenerated. Examples of these are Ishmael (probably), Esau, and Judas. But Old Testament circumcision was more than a rite performed on the flesh. The Old Testament clearly teaches that the physical rite, the sign, is not so important as the reality it signifies. It signifies that the recipient is in covenant with God: "in thee shall all the families of the earth be blessed.... I am the Almighty God... and I will make my covenant between me and thee... to be a God unto thee.... This is my covenant, ... every man child among you shall be circumcised." But though external, the sign was a sign of an internal reality: "The Lord thy God will circumcise thine heart, to love the Lord thy God;" and "Circumcise the foreskins of your hearts and be no more stiff-necked"; and so on in many places.

From this we may infer that the baptism performed by the hands of the minister is not the baptism made without hands; but that the latter, the baptism of Christ, is essentially the same as the spiritual circumcision of the Old Testament. This baptism which Christ performs "strips off the body of the flesh." The rite of circumcision stripped off literal flesh; Christ strips off metaphorical flesh—man's sinful nature.

To say this is not to denigrate the literal rite. Baptism is a sacrament just as truly as the Lord's Supper. God commands both. When at times in Israel's history circumcision fell into disuse, God called the people to repentance and obedience. It is interesting to note that pepped-up American evangelists, who look on others as lukewarm, while they make a great deal of walking up the aisle to the front to shake hands, hardly ever, and maybe never say, "Repent and be baptized." Hand-shaking evangelism does not square with apostolic teaching and practice. On one occasion a radio program struck the present writer with force and with pleasure: a Lutheran pastor urged his unconverted listeners to seek out a Lutheran church and ask for baptism. Now, the Lutheran sacramental theory may not be scriptural, but at least the pastor was following apostolic directions to the best of his knowledge.

The next phrase is "being buried with him in baptism, by and with whom also you were resurrected." This is a phrase in which Baptists delight, for it seems to picture immersion in water immediately followed by resurrection to newness of life. The Baptists, however, do not appreciate the identification of baptism with circumcision in their spiritual significance, for this authorizes the baptism of infants.

With respect to immersion it must be noted that the language here is figurative. We were not literally put into the same tomb with Christ in Gethsemane. If one thinks that the resurrection spoken of here is the literal resurrection at Christ's return, one should note that the verb is in the past tense; you *were*, not *shall be*, raised. Now it is possible that immersion in water may remind someone of burial in a tomb; but being covered with earth would be a closer analogy. Indeed, Romans 6:5 uses the figure of covering a seed with earth when it is planted. Analogies are always inexact; the literal meaning is the one we search for. Here the literal reality is Christ's vicarious, propitiatory sacrifice and our regeneration. The figures of earth or water are irrelevant.

A subsidiary point is the phrase "by whom you have also been resurrected." Some exegetes wish to translate this as, "baptism in which also you were raised." But if Paul had intended an analogy between immersion and burial, he would have said next "*out of which* you were raised." It is true that the word *baptism* is the nearest noun before the relative pronoun. It is also true that *baptism* and the relative are both masculine. Nevertheless we are raised by Christ. We are raised neither in nor by baptism. Such an idea leads to the doctrine of baptismal regeneration; and this is foreign to New Testament teaching, though the arguments will not be developed here and now. It is Christ, not baptism, who regenerates. Note that the verbs *entombed* and *resurrected* both have the prepositional prefix *with*. The first *with* can be nothing but *with* Christ; the second is surely a parallel. Hence the figure of immersion, if that were indeed Paul's meaning, would have been dropped before it was completed. This makes the Baptist interpretation unlikely.

The purpose here is not to discuss the different modes of baptism, but is simply to show that immersion is not so obviously required as some good people think. Therefore, it will be sufficient to quote a few lines from Eadie's commentary:

> The reference is plainly to the ordinance of baptism and to its spiritual meaning. We scarcely suppose that there is any reference to the mode of it; for whatever may be otherwise said in favor of immersion, it is plain that here the burial is wholly ideal—not a scenic and visible descent into an earthly or watery tomb. . . . Men may be buried in baptism without being *submerged* in water, in the same way as they may be circumcized without the spilling of blood. The entire statement is spiritual in its nature. . . . Where in Scripture is it the symbol of the world of death or the grave? It is always the means of worship—the instrument of justification. . . .

More important than the mode of baptism is "through the faith of the power of God who raised him from the dead." Our regeneration is the work of divine power, the same power that raised Christ from the dead.

In English it sounds strange to speak of the faith of Christ, or the faith of God's power. In Greek these are objective genitives: not that Christ exercises faith, or that God exercises power, but that we believe in Christ and in God's power. No doubt faith is a gift from God. It is he who causes us to believe. Then by means of our believing, God justifies us. The new life into which we have been resurrected is not only produced by the power of God, but its activity consists in believing that God's power raised Christ from the dead. Believing is the first activity produced by regeneration. We confess that Jesus is Lord and believe that God raised him from the dead. To paraphrase the verse: Christ raised us from the death of sin by causing us to believe that God's power raised him from the tomb.

2:13.   And you being dead in your transgressions and uncircumcision of the flesh, [God] made you alive with him, having shown grace [forgiven] to us with reference to all transgressions . . .

Meyer, for all his meticulous and valuable studies, in this passage, as elsewhere in I Corinthians, displays a proclivity to refer to the time of the Parousia as much as he possibly can. Thus, here, he writes, "*Sunedzōapoiēsen* [he made you alive with] is not to be taken, any more than *sunēgerthēte* [you were raised] previously, in an ethical sense, as referring to regeneration . . . but in its proper sense, and that . . . as referring to the everlasting life . . . (as an ideal possession now, but to be realized at the Parousia)." If Meyer had not explicitly denied the ethical, spiritual sense, we might be willing to speak of an ideal participation in a future everlasting life. No one denies that we shall be raised from the dead when Christ returns, and that our felicity in heaven will far exceed the present joy of salvation. But Meyer seems to deny the present blessings, viz., that we now have been raised to newness of life; our sins are now forgiven, and this is what baptism now represents as having already taken place. Is not our belief in Christ's resurrection a present fact? We would not limit the grace of God to present blessings, and picture them so vaguely as "dialectical confrontation" and "authentic living"; but neither will we transfer to the distant future the present spiritual treasures.

There are some minor points of interest in this verse. That the Colossian church was predominantly Gentile is evident from the phrase "uncircumcision of the flesh." It may seem strange to refer to the Colossians' literal uncircumcision after the previous references to spiritual circumcision two verses above. But it may be explained as a reminder of the recent extension of salvation to the Gentiles, for which the Colossians should be thankful. However, to prevent any impression that Gentiles are superior to Jews, or, more apposite to the actual conditions, that Jews are superior to Gentiles, Paul changes the second person pronoun, used twice, to the first person plural in the final clause: *you* being dead, *you made* alive, God showed grace to *us*. And since Paul, the Jew, received grace, he must have been a transgressor as truly as the Colossians had been.

This classifying of himself with all sinners, as Paul always did, may well be a part of his motivation in using the words "all transgressions." God's grace, by the merits of Christ, not by ours, expunges all our sins, all of them.

> But not for works that we have done or shall hereafter do
> Hath God decreed on sinful men salvation to bestow.

2:14.   ... having erased the bond with its stipulations that was against us, which was contrary to our [interests] and has lifted it out of our way, nailing it to the cross.

Because of the final phrase of this verse, "nailing it to the cross," some have thought that the subject of the verbal forms is Christ. This is a misapprehension. The first participle, "having erased," is parallel with "having shown grace." Thus, it was God who erased the bond, removed the obstacle, and nailed the bond to the cross. This keeps the picture consistent, for Christ nailed nothing to the cross. Therefore, we cannot say as Christ nailed something else to the cross, so he also nailed the bond. But God in a sense, by his eternal decree, nailed Christ to the cross and by so doing nailed our bond there too.

The bond is a debtor's bond, a mortgage bond, an obligation the debtor must discharge. Now, precisely what was written in the bond? To what document does Paul refer? In the Middle Ages the bond was often identified as the covenant of works with Adam. But this covenant was not a *cheirographon*, a hand written document.

Earlier Irenaeus had a fanciful explanation. Taking up the idea of the cross at the end of the verse, he said, "In a certain way, by wood we are made debtors to God, so by wood we receive the remission of our debt." *Lignum* means both *wood* and also a writing tablet. But this is too ingenious for Paul.

A more plausible view is that the mortgage is the ceremonial law.

Verse 16 lends credence to this interpretation. And in a sense it is true so far as it goes; but it is incomplete. Those, even Calvin, who restrict it to the ceremonial law apparently do so because they do not wish to abrogate morality.

However, without abrogating morality, we must understand the handwriting to be the whole Mosaic law, including the Ten Commandments. If, as is the case, the ceremonial law has been abrogated, such must be said in other passages, as for example, Acts 10 and Galatians 2:11 ff. What is meant here is the whole law, decidedly including the moral law. It is the complete law that condemns Jews and Gentiles alike. No doubt the cross atones for Jewish infractions of the sacrifices and temple ritual. But the text here says "having forgiven all your transgressions," not just ceremonial transgressions. This is what the Gentiles needed; it is also what the Jews needed.

> My sin, O the bliss of this glorious thought;
> My sin, not in part, but the whole,
> Is nailed to the cross....

This debt or guilt, which was obviously "against us" and "contrary to our" interests, God has wiped out and taken it out of our way to heaven, by Christ's death on the cross.

This is no way abrogates the Ten Commandments. The reason is that the purpose of Christ's death is not only to remove the penalty of sin from us, but also to remove sin from us. Regeneration initiates a more moral life. "If ye love me, keep my commandments." Now, the definition of sin is "any want of conformity unto or transgression of the law of God." The divine imperatives and they alone distinguish between sin and righteousness. The penalty for disobedience was paid on the cross; but this does not mean that we can now continue in sin.

2:15.   ... disarming the principalities and powers, he exposed [their shame] publicly, triumphing over them by it.

The Second Chapter of Colossians

There is a grammatical difficulty here. The first verb, a participle, is middle, not active voice, and therefore is not supposed to be transitive, and should not mean "disarming those powers." The same verb, in the middle voice, also occurs in 3:9, where it means "put off the old man," i.e., the verb means to take off one's own clothes.[1] Hence Alford and others picture Christ as having been clothed, or at least surrounded, with principalities and powers. He then laid them aside on the cross. Lightfoot writes,

> "The final act in the conflict [between Christ and Satan] began with the agony of Gethsemane; it ended with the cross of Calvary. The victory was complete. The enemy of man was defeated. The powers of evil, which had clung like a Nessus robe around his humanity, were torn off and cast aside forever."

But where in Scripture, may we ask, is there any suggestion of a poisoned robe eating at Christ's flesh?

The whole idea is too imaginative. Further the active sense fits in with the remainder of the verse much better: despoils the powers and triumphs over them.

But what about the indubitable grammatical fact that the participle is middle and not active? Well, for one thing, the middle may not have to indicate an action performed on oneself. It can also be used to denote personal interest. Then, finally, Liddell and Scott, noting that it is a deponent verb, give it the active sense: despoil.

As in the previous verse, God, not Christ, is the subject of all the verbs. This raises a question concerning the last word. *Auto* is indistinguishably masculine or neuter. Therefore it can be translated either "by it" or "by him." "Him" of course would be Christ. But more probably *auto* should refer to the cross, and be translated "by it." This gives perfectly good sense and avoids Moule's "illogical transition."

Next, to return to the middle of the verse, the word *parrēsia*, which had no bearing on the previous difficulties, means either boldly or publicly. Carson prefers the former on the ground that *publicly* would merely repeat the idea of exposure. Yet in English we speak of *exposing* evil *publicly* without being troubled by the redundancy. If then one suggests that the defeat of Satan was not

---

1. Cf. Meyer, *in loc.*

very public or evident to the people who witnessed the crucifixion, and if, too, mankind did not notice Satan falling from heaven, Paul might have replied that the principalities and powers did.

Once more modern readers need to be reminded that the universe is not restricted to rocks, trees, and stars observable by eyesight. The twentieth century is philosophically empirical and humanistic. Sensation is not only the test of truth versus falsity, but even the criterion of meaningfulness. In contradiction to this a Christian sees the universe—sees, not with his eyeballs and retina, but with his mind—as including angels, demons, spiritual beings, and sovereign over them all, the three persons of the Trinity. In the wars of religion the Christian may use *ad hominem* arguments based on humanistic presuppositions, but he must never be deceived into operating on these as if they were his own.

At this point there comes a distinct paragraph break. Paul passes from general theological teaching to the particular local difficulties in Colosse. Their difficulties were much the reverse of twentieth-century troubles. Humanism was not a major view in antiquity. The sophistic man-measure theory of Protagoras, accepted by F.C.S. Schiller in England and given a sociological twist by John Dewey in America, was rejected by most of ancient philosophers and of course ignored by the common populace. The latter, if not the philosophers, believed in demons and angels. In fact this was their error: they believed too much in them. Thus their deviations from Christian truth went in the opposite direction from present-day opposition. Yet if modern pragmatism, positivism, and existentialism escape Paul's condemnation in these next verses, there are nonetheless religiously inclined persons today who fall into somewhat the same errors. Other religiously inclined persons push Paul's admonitions beyond his intentions. Human nature finds it hard not to turn aside either to the right or to the left. It is hard neither to add nor subtract. To avoid such fleshly inclinations, one should try to understand Paul's meaning with precision.

> 2:16.   Accordingly let no one judge you in respect of food and drink, or in the matter of a feast, a new moon, or sabbaths.

The Second Chapter of Colossians

To most people this verse must seem as an extremely trivial application of the sublime principles just enumerated. Another way of looking at it is that if these details are subsumed under such sublime principles they must be more important than one would ordinarily think.

The reference to food and drink, though the Mosaic regulations on drink are far less numerous, is an admonishment that these laws are abrogated and especially that they contribute nothing to the Christian life. Next come feast days and new moons. Aside from weddings, birthdays, and other such private family gatherings, which are not envisaged in this verse, these are feasts enjoined by law and listed in Leviticus 23. There was the weekly Sabbath, the Passover, and toward the end of the chapter, the Feast of Tabernacles. It is to be noted that some of the dates mentioned here indicate that Sabbaths were not confined to the seventh day of the week. Verse 24 establishes a Sabbath on the first day of the seventh month. Therefore it would not usually fall on Saturday. Similarly verse 39 also dates a Sabbath. Pentecost gave rise to a controversy on this very point. The Pharisees dated the Passover Sabbath regardless of the day of the week; the Sadducees took the opposite view.

Perhaps because of the Pharisaic multiplication of rules for the Sabbath, and in our day because of antagonism toward the Puritans and Covenanters, Sabbath has a lugubrious reputation. But for the pre-exilic Jews at least, these were joyous days of rest. The Sabbath was made for man, to give him rest from labor and a day to praise the Lord. Instead of viewing the restrictions as depressing, the women could take pleasure in the prohibition of cooking.

Later on, as was said, the Pharisees added ridiculous prescriptions to the Sabbath, and their theology made all the feasts meritorious for salvation. The sinner must earn his salvation, if not wholly by his own obedience, at least by obedience plus mercy.

It is in the light of these conditions, so different from our own, that we must understand the passage. But though superstitious observance of minute Sabbath regulations is not the besetting sin of America, or even of American church people, Paul's injunctions apply today also. The food laws cause us no trouble, but feasts and new moons do. Our Covenanter and Puritan forefathers refused to celebrate Christmas and Easter because of their serious acceptance of this paragraph. Nowhere in the Bible is a celebration of Christmas given a warrant. Nor Easter. The resurrection is to be celebrated every week. A yearly Easter is a superstitious invention. More recently the liberal churches have attempted to celebrate Pentecost. Even in the Reformed Presbyterian Church Evangelical Synod, on a recent Lord's Day morning, a preacher called for the revival of the church calendar. This is the old Roman road. Even so early as the fifth century Augustine groaned under the load of special holy days. These are what Paul forbids.

The most disturbing element in this verse is the Sabbath, or the Sabbaths. Admittedly the plural is sometimes used for the singular in the New Testament. Matthew 12:1 and 28:1 are examples. The second instance of the word in 28:1 means *week*. Hence no conclusion can be certainly drawn from the plural word alone in our passage. But if this "no conclusion" prevents us from deciding that *Sabbaths* mean special days, it also prevents the conclusion that the regular weekly Sabbath is meant. What needs emphasis, however, in our contemporary unfamiliarity with ancient Jewish customs, is their celebration of Sabbaths on various days of the week.

That these special celebrations were now prohibited, but that the weekly Sabbath is still required, the following argument aims to show.

First, the Sabbath is a creation ordinance: it is not a Mosaic innovation. God not only rested from his work of creation, he blessed the day and sanctified it (Gen. 2:3). This is such an obvious and tremendous consideration that the reduction of the Sabbath to nothing more than a Mosaic ceremony is incredible. What can antisabbatarians make of Genesis 2:3?

It is often said that there is no mention of the Sabbath before the Exodus from Egypt. Note, however, that before the time of Abraham the account is sparse on all points. For example, the law of monogamous marriage is not mentioned, though Christ referred to it as imposed at creation. Also, there is no mention of sacrifices from the time of Abel to Noah, nor from Genesis 47:1 till after the Exodus, a period of four hundred years. There is no mention of the Sabbath from Joshua to I Kings inclusive; and yet this was a post-

Mosaic period. Even Psalms and Proverbs do not mention the Sabbath with any frequency. Hence sparcity, with reference to sacrifice, marriage, and the Sabbath, does not prove their non-existence.

Sparcity, furthermore, is not silence. There are passages in Genesis which can be explained only on the basis of a previous Sabbath law. The word itself may not be used, but note the seven-day divisions in Genesis 7:4, 10 and 8:10, 12. Even before this, Cain and Abel brought their sacrifices "in the process of time," more literally "at the end of days." The only reference to days so far is the seven days of creation. Then later, Genesis 17:12 and 21:4 indicate, if not the Sabbath, at least the weekly division of days, eight days counting both ends. Genesis 29:27–28 again indicate a division of time into sevens. Since seven times twenty-four is incommensurable with both the year and the month, Laban's dishonesty is evidence of a creation ordinance.

Incidentally the division of time into weeks and so observed by the heathen nations, must be, since it cannot be justified astronomically, a reminiscense of creation.

That the weekly Sabbath was not first instituted by the Ten Commandments, Moses himself makes clear. Exodus 16—the Decalogue comes in Exodus 20—without any mention of inaugurating a new custom, but rather giving the impression of something already known, indicates that the Sabbath is a day of rest. Note particularly Exodus 16:23, "This is that which the Lord hath said, Tomorrow is the rest of the holy sabbath . . ." (cf. verses 25–26). Now, of course, the Lord said this in verse 5; but far from indicating a novel institution, then and there decreed for the first time, verse 4 speaks of it as a law. God will now test the Israelites by a law already known. Had it been a new law, the wording would have had to be different. Furthermore, the Mosaic law itself, the Ten Commandments, indeed the Fourth Commandment, says, "Remember." During the slavery in Egypt, the people had probably been forced to work every day. It is not likely that the Egyptians were Sabbatarians. Over the centuries the Israelites had perhaps half forgotten the Law. Now, on Mt. Sinai, God says, "Remember."

The opponents no doubt reply, "God at Sinai promulgated a new law and told them to remember it henceforth." But the division of time into weeks, and the revelation in Genesis 2:3, are ruinous to such a reply.

If the Fourth Commandment was newly instituted in the desert, how can one avoid inconsistency without regarding the other nine also as new? Now, there is no mention of any law against murder in the first four chapters of Genesis. Yet Cain clearly knew that murder was forbidden. He also knew that God had sanctified the Sabbath.

For this reason the Ten Commandments must be regarded as the moral law, in the words of the Catechism, "summarily comprehended." Is it not utterly incongruous to think of a temporary ceremonial regulation embedded in the Decalogue? If all mankind, not the Jews only, are obligated to worship the one true God, to avoid images and profanity, are they not also obligated to sanctify the Sabbath forever? A negative answer is utter absurdity.

Conversely if Colossians 2:14 is understood as blotting out all written ordinances, then how can the other nine ordinances, written by the hand of God, still be in effect? If it be said that the New Testament reenacts the other nine, but not the fourth, we demur on the latter assertion, and accuse the reenactment of producing a contradiction with the verse in Colossians.

The conclusion is therefore that Paul does not abrogate the Lord's Day, but that he forbids the celebration of saints' days, Easter, and Christmas.

There is one further defense of the integrity of the Ten Commandments, one that brings us back to the present text. The context speaks of food and drink, feasts, and new moons. All this is ceremonial. Then are not the Sabbaths, here condemned, ceremonial Sabbaths, and not the creation ordinance?

Alford, in opposition to the Presbyterian, Covenanter, and Puritan principle, asserted, "We may observe that if the ordinance of the Sabbath had been *in any form* [italics his] of lasting obligation on the Christian church, it would have been impossible for the Apostle to have spoken thus."

This is a mere supposition about how the apostle ought to write. But there is a more likely supposition. Given the Jewish milieu and Paul's training, he could have written these words on the reasonable assumption that no one would ever have thought of an attack on the Ten Commandments.

2:17.   ... which things are shadows of the future, but the body of Christ.

There are two or three puzzles in this verse, and its last phrase was translated literally to indicate one of these.

The initial relative pronoun causes no difficulty; it refers to ceremonial observances. But the verb *is* (Greek uses the singular where English requires the plural) needs consideration. Meyer repeatedly insists that the present tense, denoting Paul's own time, requires the future to be future to Paul, and that therefore the things to come, do not come before the Messianic age. The ceremonial shadows are not shadows of the present gospel realities, but of the millennium. Were the shadows shadows of the gospel, Paul would have used the past tense.

This sounds like a strong argument; yet neither Lightfoot, Moule, nor Carson take any note of it. They all take *is* to be *was*. Eadie, on the contrary, says the apostle employs *esti* in the present, not because as Meyer argues, the blessings are yet future, but either because he gives a definition, or because the apostle transports himself ideally into the past period of ritualism. This is no knockdown, drag-out argument; but it produces much better sense.

"The body of Christ" is also puzzling. Of course, one must insert a verb to complete the meaning. So we say, "The body is Christ's." One cannot say, "The body is Christ." *Christ* in this verse is genitive, not nominative. But what is the figure of speech? Does *shadow* mean a rough sketch and the *body* a finished work of art? Meyer will not have it that *skia* (shadow) can possibly mean sketch (*skiagraphia*). So he has the Messianic glory casting the shadow of Christ's body on the Old Testament, indeed upon the New Testament too. Moule wants to identify the body of Christ as the church. While this concedes too much to the high-church Anglicans, Greek Orthodox, and Romanists, his contrast between the shadow and the substance or "real thing" is a good one: the reality foreshadowed in Moses belonged to Christ. A concrete example would be Passover contrasted with the Lord's Supper, circumcision contrasted with baptism, and the sacrifice of lambs as a type of the death of Christ himself.

> **2:18.   Let no one rob you, willingly, by humility and a worshipping of angels, which things he has seen, going into detail, in vain being conceited by the mind of his flesh.**

This translation is intentionally crude because it aims to preserve for the English reader some of the difficulties of the original. A smooth translation would beg the questions, for even the first two commas above are themselves a sort of interpretation beyond the text. The clauses require more.

The first verb is the least difficult. In Greek it can mean to give an adverse decision, to deprive of a rightful prize, and one commentator makes it: "Let no one usurp the position of an umpire against you." The King James word *reward* is not in the text, and the simple verb *rob* seems satisfactory.

The next word, *willingly*, or just plain *willing*, is more difficult. To what is it attached? Should we say, "Let no man be willing to rob you?" Hardly, for no one can prevent a thief from attempting voluntary thievery.

The "willing" cannot be attached to *you* Colossians for two reasons: First, willing is singular and you is plural; second, hardly anybody needs to be told, "Do not willingly be robbed." The next verb and two participles are also singular, and must refer to a false teacher—the *mēdeis*, the "no one" at the beginning of the verse. It does not follow that Paul had one nameable person in mind. It was just no one or someone.

But then, in what respect is the robber willing? Of course thieves are always willing. It is rather unnecessary therefore to say with one commentator, "Let no one on purpose defraud you." In fact this defrauder is not deliberately defrauding you. He does not rob you on purpose, at least not usually, not consciously. The idea of volition attaches to the next two nouns. The King James, with a change of one word, expresses the sense well: "Let no man beguile you of your reward in a voluntary humility and worshipping of angels." The voluntary part consists in his invention, beyond any biblical revelation, of a new religion: the worship of angels. This interpretation is supported by verse 23 below. The direct force of the *willingly* stops with the mention of angel worship, and can only in an extenuated sense apply to the verbs following *which things*.

Though the text deals only with the voluntary invention of religious rites, there is occasionally a voluntary attempt by super-humble people to dominate by a show of humility. To delay a decision that seems to be forming against them, they will ask the group to pause for prayer. This is a disconcerting tactic, but a conscientious Christian must not allow these people to have their way.

Although angel worship as such is not a prominent sin in this century, other humanly invented religions abound. Against them we must observe the warning of this verse. But the exegete must consider angels.

Now it is true that angels are superior in power and mind to men. God has used them in remarkable ways. Stephen in his great speech says that Christ with an angel was in the wilderness with Moses. Also Christ will return to earth accompanied by a host of angels. But however superior these beings are, and with whatever powers and functions God has endowed them, they are not to be worshiped. Revelation 19:10 is not the only verse that prohibits the worship of anyone other than God. Not only were the Gentiles in the habit of worshiping many gods, but according to the noncanonical writings some Jews, presumably for the most part of the Dispersion, also engaged in angel worship. The early Christian writers, Origen and Clement for example, witness to such Jewish practices.

But how pitiful is the worship of angels when contrasted with the sublime Christology of chapter 1! It robs the worshiper of a great reward.

Now, if angels are not to be worshiped, neither may saints. And if God alone receives our prayers, Mariolatry is an inexcusable sin. There is only one Mediator, and he is not the virgin mother of Jesus. Theodoret reports that in his day the Colossians built a temple in honor of the archangel Michael. Paul therefore had good reason for his warning; but it was very little heeded throughout the Middle Ages. It still remains in that synagogue of Satan from which the Reformers excluded themselves and were excluded.

The second half of the verse has its difficulties too. Instead of the words "which things he has seen," some manuscripts read, "which things he has not seen." The *which things* are those just mentioned, at least those of this verse and maybe those of the previous two verses also. But did the false teacher see them or did he not? The negative makes easy sense: he doesn't know what he is talking about, he has not seen—well, what has he not seen? Angels perhaps? On the other hand, if the false teacher has had visions, the words make good sense without the negative; he saw these things in his visions. Of course we cannot be sure that such a man had seen any visions at all.

The next word *embateuōn* may help in the decision, though this word too has caused the commentators difficulty. The King James translation *intruding* and Lightfoot's *invading* are not the best possibilities. Even so, we reject the latter's suggestion that "there was perhaps some corruption in the text prior to all existing authorities." His conjectural emendation is indeed conjectural.

There is, however, a meaning of *embateuōn* that is not only supported by the lexicons, but also fits the situation psychologically, viz., *going into detail*. Muddle-headed thinkers, and some not so muddle-headed, occasionally become so enamored of their theories that they project them into unwarranted detail. For example, Immanuel Kant, to whom Paul's accusations could never literally apply, was so enamored of balanced schemes that he developed twelve categories in groups of three which, since his arguments are remarkably poor, are supported only by his aesthetic sensibilities. Or, to return closer to Paul's time, Proclus, the last of the Neoplatonists, invented a world of unintelligible distinctions. So too, men of small superstitious minds invent ritual niceties and complex taboos in which the Grand Imperial Wizard and Potentate with his subjects take great comfort.

Why then should not Paul say, "vainly conceited by the mind of his flesh"? One could also put the comma after vainly and read it as,

100

"vainly going into detail, conceited," etc. In English the word *vain* has acquired a connotation a little different from its original meaning. If we call a man vain, we mean he is conceited. But the meaning in the text—and how the two are connected is easily seen—continues in the English phrase "he tried in vain"; that is, his efforts were useless. Since men beset with *vanity* are not the only ones who may act *in vain*, Paul adds *phusioumenos*, "conceited," to *eikē*, "in vain."

He is conceited by reason of his fleshly mind. The word *flesh* is sometimes used literally, but here it is figurative. "The world, the flesh, and the devil" is a phrase where the word *flesh* clearly carries the connotation of sin. People who worship angels, kiss the big toe of St. Peter's statue in Philadelphia, and pray to the virgin Mary have sinful minds.

2:19.   ... and not holding on to the head, from which the whole body, supported and united by its ligaments and bonds, grows the growth of God.

Once again Paul refers back to his Christology. False teachers do not hold on to Christ: they hold on to angels and Mary. But Christ is the head, and without him the body is dead and cannot grow.

The difficulties in this verse are minimal. The first is that the word *head* is feminine and the word *which* is masculine. The change in gender could be intended to place emphasis on Christ. One could also argue that neuter pronouns—for *ou* is neuter as well as masculine—often follow feminine antecedents. The translation would then be, "the head, from which. ... " This grammatical point bears on a misunderstanding of Ephesians 2:8, where Arminians sometimes, by a fallacious argument as well as by an ignorance of grammar, try to avoid viewing *faith* as a gift of God. *Faith* and *head* can both take neuter relatives; and here it seems better to use the neuter, for it refers to Christ in his office as head, rather than in his personal attributes. Furthermore, *kephalēn* is immediately prior, and the word *Christ* takes us back to verse 17.

Meyer seems to take *aphōn* as nerves, rather than ligaments.

101

Lightfoot connects the term with *nourishment*, and then runs riot with Hippocrates, Plato, Aristotle, and Galen. But the words themselves do not have these specific meanings. Furthermore, the language is figurative and therefore the plain words *ligaments* and *bonds* are satisfactory.

The *body* is presumably the church, the body of Christians. The same figure occurs in I Corinthians 12:12–14, 27, though Christ is not there called the head. But does the church grow, or does the individual grow? Of course, this is a false disjunction. They both grow. The present verse says the body, the church as a whole, grows; Ephesians 4:14–15 specifies the "children," that is, the individuals. In both cases the growth is the growth caused by God. No evangelist, not even the apostle Paul, made the church grow. Paul planted the word; Apollos watered it; but God gave the increase.

> **2:20,21.   If you died with Christ from the elements of the world, why do you, as if you were living in the world, submit to decrees [such as] touch not, taste not, handle not?**

Verses 18, 19 are a sort of transition from straightforward theology to exhortation. Certainly 20–23, or at least 20–22, are exhortation.

The first two words are better "if you died," rather than "if you are dead." Some exegetes wish to connect this with baptism: baptism is like a death. They refer back to verses 12–13. But the figurative language—for we neither died physically nor spiritually: spiritually we became alive—does not require a sacramentarian view of baptism. Certainly this verse refers to our turning from sin, which baptism pictures as a washing away of defilement; and this event needs the aorist tense (simple past) rather than the perfect.

Note then, what we became dead to, or from. By our connection with Christ we became dead to the elements of the world. This word *elements* occurred above in verse 8. The context prevents the word *elements* from meaning the elements of the physical universe, the scientific principles of earth, air, fire, and water. Nor will it allow them to be spirits or demons, as Moule seems to think. Rather these elements are moral and religious principles which appear good to those minds that do not submit to God's revealed word. They are certain worldly decrees. To such decrees or taboos a Christian should not submit. If we died with Christ and were freed from the popular opinions of the world, and in this case particularly from the taboos of some sect, why should we live according to such standards? That Paul means moral opinions and standards, rather than either atoms or spirits, is clear from the example he immediately appends: touch not, taste not, handle not.

The King James translation is a proper one. Commentators point out that the verb *touch* can mean to touch food. So it can. *Taste*, of course, requires food and drink. *Handle* can also refer to food. But then *aptō* does not always refer to food; and *thigganō* can mean *attack* as well as *handle*, or *handle food*. Doubtless Paul has foods chiefly in mind; but this must be determined by the context. The verbs themselves mean simply, touch, taste, handle. And even if Paul had food chiefly in mind, we cannot exclude from his thought the touching or handling of things the Mosaic law made unclean. In fact, the verse is a warning against all asceticism. In conjunction with other passages this one condemns priestly celibacy. In fact, *aptō*, in addition to references to food, also includes the conjugal relationship. So, elsewhere, Paul condemns those who forbid marriage. Lightfoot argues that if Paul had marriage in mind, he would not have passed over it in a single word. But if, as Lightfoot himself asserts, "the apostle disparagingly repeats the prohibition of the false teachers in their own words," "rabbinical passages quoted ... exactly ... not only the spirit, but even the form," there was no need for him to enter upon a special discussion of marriage.

Then, finally, some exegetes try to find an ascending or descending hierarchy in the three verbs. The first is the strongest, or perhaps the weakest, the more general, or the more particular; and the third is the reverse of these. Such bright ideas are highly ingenious.

2:22. ... all of which are toward destruction in use, according to the commandments and teachings of men?

The Second Chapter of Colossians

This verse completes the sentence, a question, that began in verse 20. The translation above does not disguise a difficulty. One interpretation would be: Do not subject yourselves to the maxim and its reason, viz., "Touch not... these things which by using them lead to your own destruction"; for this maxim is a human superstition. That is to say, the maxim which Paul condemns runs from *Touch not* to *in use*; then Paul's comment is that the whole phrase in human folly.

Another interpretation is: "Do not be subject to the maxim, 'Touch not,' for I Paul tell you these foods are simply digested when you eat them, and the maxim is a human invention.' A third possibility might be: "Don't be subject, for as I Corinthians 6:13 says, God will destroy both our stomachs and the foods we eat by resurrecting us in glorified bodies."

To sort out these interpretations, and any other variations, we may begin with what is least questionable. "All of which" most probably refers to foods and drinks. It would also include marriage, since this too is destroyed at death and does not continue in heaven. The phrase "All of which" is not so likely to mean, "All such maxims." Rather, all things subsumed under the maxim.

Second, the maxim with its three verbs makes a neat aphorism. It is complete in itself. More would spoil it. Therefore the first half of verse 22 is more likely to be Paul's parenthetical remark than a quotation from the ascetics. This conclusion is strengthened in another way also. If the ascetics had argued, "Don't touch, because all these things destroy you," Paul would have agreed to the validity of the argument. He would have agreed that one should not eat anything that would destroy the eater. He surely would have said, "Don't use heroin." But in this case he would have opposed the ascetics by an argument different from that of the text. His words would have been, "But these things do not destroy you: they were forbidden only as ritual regulations." Paul here opposes not harmful foods but ritual regulations, both Mosaic and the greater number of later Jewish additions. Paul elsewhere (Romans, I Corinthians, Galatians) rejects ritual observances as inimical to justification by faith alone. They make a saving relationship to Christ impossible. This is such a dominant note in Paul's music that there is nothing strange in finding it here. The word *phthora* may seem strange in designating *digestion*. But the food is *consumed* and *destroyed* in the stomach. Digestion can easily be taken, must be taken, as one form of "corruption." So far as the lexical meaning is concerned, the Greek commentators—and Greek was their mother tongue—were unmistakably explicit in their reference to the lower alimentary canal.

The harsh translation at the beginning may now be paraphrased: "... why do you live according to the worldly ascetic principle, 'Touch not, taste not, handle not.' The things you eat are simply consumed. The maxim is a purely human contrivance." And may the commentator, if not the exegete, add: "such as the celebration of Christmas, the worship of the 'saints,' and the celibacy of priests and nuns."

The next verse (2:23) also presents us with difficulties. Some of the single words, in this verse and in the preceding verses, are either very rare in Greek literature or even hapaxlegomena—used only once in the New Testament. Their meaning must be ascertained with great care. Since crabbed translation may by now have become tedious, here are given some of the standard translations.

> 2:23. *King James:* Which things have indeed a shew of wisdom in will worship, and humility, and neglecting of the body; not in any honor to the satisfying of the flesh.

> *New American Standard Version:* These are matters which have, to be sure, the appearance of wisdom in self-made religion and self-abasement and severe treatment of the body, but are of no value against fleshly indulgence.

> *Revised Standard Version:* These things have indeed an appearance of wisdom in promoting rigor of devotion and self-abasement and severity to the body, but they are of no value in checking the indulgence of the flesh.

The Second Chapter of Colossians

On the last phrase a footnote in the Revised Standard Version says, "are of no value, serving only to indulge the flesh."

> *New International Version:* **Such regulations indeed have an appearance of wisdom, with their self-imposed worship, their false humility, and their harsh treatment of the body, but they lack any value in restraining sensual indulgence.**

The King James is a good translation. The others are not. They may be good paraphrases; they may make the meaning clearer; but as such they are interpretations rather than translations. For example, the last four words of the verse may in other contexts mean sensual indulgence; but since *flesh* in the New Testament connotes sinful tendencies in general, the last four words can mean the gratification of spiritual pride. A translation should say *flesh*. But to state what *flesh* means in this passage is not translation: it is interpretation. Therefore the New International Version is not a good translation. I would like to insist on this, in opposition to the methods of many modern "translators." First, observing fasting and food laws is not sensual indulgence: it is precisely the reverse. Second, only five verses back Paul referred to the *mind* of the flesh, i.e., the fleshly mind. II Corinthians 1:12 speaks of fleshly wisdom. Hence the words of this verse refer to spiritual pride rather than to sensual orgies. The opponents are ascetics.

Strict rules of translation do not prohibit interpretations and commentaries—or this one would never have been written. But to the best of our ability, we should understand what we are doing. Conscious paraphrasing of Xenophon's *Anabasis* or *Memorabilia* is bad scholarship. Conscious interpretation of the Scriptures in translations is sin. Unconscious interpretation is deplorable, even if not wholly eradicable. There is always some in putting one language into another. Let an American who knows French well try to translate into French the simple sentence, John runs to school. Jean court à l'école? No!

The Second Chapter of Colossians

Very well: "Which things," i.e., the various ascetic practices, look as if they were wise and good. This superficial appearance consists in the fact that the taboo is a voluntary decision, a personal decision, without any scriptural warrant. There is no command to celebrate Pentecost; but would not God be pleased if I did more than he required? So, I shall abstain from oysters, and beef on Friday, and God will for that reason add merits to my heavenly bank account. How humble I am, thus to add to God's minimal requirements. I am more humble than he demands me to be. I shall, no, I *will* treat my body severely. If I go to bed at nine o'clock, I will rise at midnight for an hour of prayer. If I can't whip myself very well over my back, my brother monks and I will form a circle and flagellate each other. These things have a reputation for wisdom, in their will-worship and humility. Of course it is a false humility as the New International Version says, but the word *false* is not in the text.

The context is asceticism. The terms *body* and *flesh* are not synonymous. Gratification of the flesh does not, and cannot here mean sensual orgies. It refers to conceited humility. Such a humility has an appearance of piety, until its true character is discovered.

Now comes the word *apheidia*, in parallel with the preceding two nouns. This word can mean a hardening, as an athlete hardens his body when training for a prize fight. It also refers to exposure to hardship and danger. This raises an interesting point. Is such hardening of the body something sinful, as the text seems to say? Did not Paul deliberately give his body "a black eye"—"I treat it roughly, I bring it under subjection" (I Cor. 9:27)? Then why does he condemn such ascetic training here? This difficulty is compounded in the two preceding nouns. The plausible but deceitful appearance of wisdom arises through three factors. First, will-worship, i.e., the personal decision to do what God has not required. Clearly all such is condemned by Paul. The second is humility. The ascetics' humility is indeed conceit; but equally certain is it that Paul does not condemn all humility as he condemns all will-worship. The third is this hardening, subjecting, severe treatment of the body. Yet by example this is what Paul recommends. The difficulty seems to have escaped the notice of most commentators.

Can Paul possibly mean that bodily hardship is of no value whatever? Bodily exercise is of little profit, but *apheidia somatos* is of value, is it not?

The contrast between Paul's practice of bringing the body into subjection and his condemnation of "severe treatment" here is best explained by noting the reverse parallelism between the two parts of the verse, viz., a reputation for wisdom in humility and hardening of the body, versus no honor with reference to fleshly indulgence. Humility and hardship give asceticism a good reputation, but a good reputation does not come by means of fleshly indulgence. Remember that "fleshly indulgence" does not mean sensual orgies. The argument is confined to the limits of asceticism. Fleshly indulgence means something like conceit. Hence beating the body for the purpose of surviving the hardships of evangelization is to be commended; but hardening the body in response to nonbiblical principles is spiritual pride and dishonorable.

Now, to finish with the verse and also to close the chapter, may we append a translation—with as little interpretation as translation allows—which at least makes the interpretation probable.

> **2:23.** ... **which things are things having a reputation (*logos*) of wisdom by will-worship and humility and severe treatment of the body,[2] not by any honor with reference to the gratification of the flesh.**

2. For an official description of a Romish saint, see Eadie, footnote *in loc.*, p. 211.

The Third Chapter

3:1.   If therefore you were raised with Christ, seek things above, where Christ is seated on the right (hand) of God;

Finally in this difficult epistle there is a verse easy to translate and which therefore presents minimal problems of interpretation. The truncated argument begins with the premise that Christians are such because God has resurrected them to newness of life. With other implicit premises the conclusion is that we ought to seek things above. What things? They are things in heaven where Christ is seated. These things may include, indeed must at least include, a study of the nature and function of angels, from which study we shall know not to worship them. But angels are by no means all. The phrase itself, "things above," is inclusive. It would be difficult to list all the interests of heaven. Their prominence in the popular mind varies with time and place. Angel worship was a real danger in Colosse. In this twentieth century the opposite is the more pressing problem: the denial of angels. Our present task is to defend and propagate a spiritual view of reality in opposition to an excessive, even an exclusive emphasis on corporeal reality, such as that found in behaviorism, logical positivism, and humanism. Christians must believe in angels and demons. God himself is a spirit and has not a body like men (Children's Catechism). We certainly believe in life after death, in heaven and hell. Our whole philosophy contrasts violently with present day secularism. Then too, with respect to the immediate concerns of our everyday life, a spiritual view will give us an evaluation of food, economics, politics, housing, pollution, bureaucracies, quite different from the views of the liberal establishment.

But above all, the greatest "thing" above, that is, the most important object of contemplation, is the Father, with Christ at his right hand; and also the Spirit, though he is not mentioned in this verse. After visiting several congregations and various Bible conferences, even the most evangelical type, one must wonder how many Christians spend much time thinking about the Trinity. The psychological sermons may stress interpersonal relationships of ordinary life; but how often do we hear a lecture on the interpersonal relationships in the Trinity? Yet the doctrine of the Trinity is one of those "things" we should seek and contemplate.

It may be of interest to note one misinterpretation of this verse. Alford refers the verb *sunēgerthēte* to baptism: "That we may not make the mistakes so commonly made of interpreting *sunēgerthēte* in an ethical sense and thereby stultifying the sentence—for if the participation were an ethical one, what need to exhort them to its ethical realization?" However, the last reference to baptism was ten verses back; in these ten verses the subject is certainly everyday moral conduct; the context in the remainder of chapter 3 is also Christian morality. Hence, Alford's interpretation is too imaginative. His objection to the ethical interpretation is also poor. Paul frequently exhorts Christians on the basis of what they already know. Work out your own salvation, he says in another place, for it is God who worked in you, and the work he began, he will finish.

3:2, 3.   . . . think about things above, not things on the earth; for you died, and your life has been hidden with Christ in God.

The Third Chapter of Colossians

Has not Paul said it clearly enough in the first verse? Must he repeat it in verse 2? But it is not just repetition. The thought itself is made more explicit. Verse 1 says, "Seek." This verse says, "Think." It is very likely that many Christians, upon being told to seek, would be perplexed as to what to do. *Think* is more specific. They are to think about what the Bible says and study out its meaning.

The King James translation, "set your affections" is not a particularly good one. Paul is not recommending anything emotional. Rather he tells us to think, to meditate, to consider. Then he adds explicitly what was only implied in the first verse, "not earthly concerns." That husbands are to love their wives and provide for their children is a Christian duty that Paul commands in the next chapter; but not even family life, much less Olympic games and political ambition, should be our main concern.

The reason is that "you died." The verb is not *you are dead*. This latter usually refers to being dead in sin. But "you died" indicates a point in past time, not a continuing state of being dead. Sacramentarians like Alford and Lightfoot wish to refer this to the act of baptism. F. F. Bruce is completely evasive. Perhaps the moment of time could be located at our regeneration. But more likely Paul is thinking of the crucifixion, when in our representative we died to the law, being crucified with Christ (Gal. 2:19-20). "Nevertheless I live," and this new life is hid with Christ in God. Hidden, no doubt, because the Christian's motives are an enigma to the worldly.

Lightfoot is surely mistaken and his concessive clause reveals it: "When you sank under the baptismal water [though infant children of the covenant do not], you disappeared forever to the world. You rose again, it is true, but you rose only to God." Thus the event of baptism gives a picture that does not fit Paul's wording. Rising from immersion is an event that any unbeliever can witness. But "yet not I, but Christ liveth in me" is not observable.

In Galatians Paul said, Christ lives in me. Here he says, I live in Christ. These two expressions mean the same thing. One could not be true without the other.

3:4.   When Christ, who is your life, appears, then you shall also appear with him in glory.

Just as an old monk tried to justify retirement in a monastery by the idea of hiddenness, a more recent commentator is equally mistaken by supposing that the influence of Christ in our lives, at first hidden from the world, eventually makes itself apparent to the non-Christians around us. Now, while it is true that eventually the unregenerate community may notice a Christian's changed life, particularly if he had been openly scandalous, as an interpretation of this verse it is impossible nonsense. It has nothing to do with our example to unbelievers. The text says, "then shall you appear with him in glory." The reference is to the Parousia.

While a commentary could well omit the mention of I John 3:1-2, yet the glory of Christ's return is so much our hope, whether we live in the first or sixteenth century of martyrdom, or whether we live in a century of drab routine, or whether we live in danger of a nuclear holocaust—Christ's return is so much our hope that the commentator cannot refrain from reminding his readers that "the world does not know us because it did not know him. Beloved, we are the sons of God now, and it has not yet become evident what we shall be. We know that when he appears, we shall be like him because we shall see him as he is."

> **3:5,6   Accordingly, put the earthly parts to death: fornication, impurity, emotion, evil desire, and greed, which is idolatry; because of which things the wrath of God comes upon the sons of disobedience.**

In defending the ethical as opposed to the sacramentarian interpretation of verse 1, emphasis was placed on the ethical subject matter of the context. This view is not weakened by the eschatalogical note in verse 4. Paul immediately returns to the matter of morality.

The metaphorical wording of this verse sounds strange to us. *Melē* literally refers to feet, arms, head, ears—the parts of the body. Here Paul speaks of several sins as members or parts of the sinful man. In apposition to the word *parts* are the specific sins Paul has in mind. He may be using these only as examples, but at any rate they are fornication and so on. There may be a logical order among them. Fornication is the most specific and definite. Impurity is wider and more generic. Perhaps emotion is still more inclusive. But at this point the increasing generality is hard to follow. Perhaps evil desire is wider than emotion or passion; but greed seems as restricted as fornication. However, since greed is equated with idolatry, whereas fornication and the others are not, maybe Paul meant it in a very wide sense; for example, fornication may be a kind of greed. It will be noticed too that whereas all passion or emotion is condemned, not all desire is. Some desires are good. Therefore Paul specifies evil desires.

The wrath of God is visited upon those who commit these sins. Moule, with a nonbiblical view of the nature of God, asserts, "It is at any rate clear that the implications of the Gospel do not for one moment leave room for *orgē* as God's *vindictive anger.*" The term *vindictive* is a device of propaganda depending on its pejorative connotation. The proper term is *vindicatory*. At any rate the Bible, too frequently to suit sinners, speaks of God's wrath. Does not Paul in Romans 1:18 warn us of God's wrath?

God's wrath comes "upon the sons of disobedience." Though Tischendorf deleted these words, and the Aland text brackets them, the objective textual evidence in their favor is overwhelming. The subjectivity of Lightfoot is patent; and Metzger's defense for bracketing them is weak.

3:7. . . . in which [sins] you also once walked when you lived in these.

"In which sins" is a better interpretation than "among which people." The "in which" and the "in these" surely have the same reference; "to walk" is an expression denoting one's conduct rather than one's associates; furthermore the neuter fits in better with the following verse than does the masculine.

This reference to the past sinful life of the Colossians is not condemnatory. Of course the sins are to be condemned. But the next verse is a contrast that makes the whole commendatory. Of course

113

the Colossians are not perfectly sinless; but they are saints and as such can profit by exhortation.

> **3:8   But now you too cast off all these, [viz.,] wrath, passion [or, anger], depravity [or, malice], blasphemy, shameful speech from your mouth.**

The repentant sinner, the sinner who has "changed his mind," may indeed regret his past sins and be ashamed of them, but they do not weigh heavily upon him. The Colossians could thank God and rejoice that he had delivered them from such a life. Yet we remain sinners still and need to be reminded of what to avoid.

Paul specifies wrath. The same word in verse 6 designated the wrath of God. God's unemotional wrath of justice is not sin; man's passion or anger is. Wrath and passion, or anger and indignation, are two elastic terms and the boundary between them is difficult to determine. They are used colloquially, and Eadie's attempt to give them distinguishable meanings is somewhat imaginative. Depravity (*kakian*) like the English word *evil* is a very general term. Blasphemy is not only speaking evil of God, but of men also. The Greek word is *blasphēmia*; a good English translation would be *slander*. Whereas slander is directed against a person, shameful speech is again more general. It would include dirty jokes.

These are the sins the Colossians have now or are now putting off. The verb is imperative. Paul is issuing a command. Note that the text says, "you also." Who else, then? The epistle was of course addressed to the Colossians; but the message is addressed to all Christians. The Colossians, though not because of this one word "also," but rather because they understood the apostolic authority of Paul's letters, made copies (cf. 4:16 below) and sent them to other congregations. Similarly the Romans and Corinthians must also have made copies, so that before the century ended every congregation, or nearly every one, had a copy of the complete canon.

> **3:9.   Do not lie to one another, since you have put off the old man with his practices, ...**

The Third Chapter of Colossians

The command not to lie hardly needs any explanation, though one may remark with Eadie that falsehood is contrary to a God who is truth itself. Paul, however, gives a reason: lying is a part of the old man and his practices, which old man Christians have discarded.

Moule denies that the old man is simply one's old bad character. He tries to find in the expression, and the following reference to the new man, a corporate association first with Adam and second with Christ. Well, no doubt the Christian casts off the old Adamic nature; but in view of the catalogue of sins here, it is more likely that Paul is thinking of practices and conduct rather than of the ideas in Romans 5:12–21. When, further, Moule drags in his favorite notion of baptismal incorporation, we simply cannot agree.

> 3:10. ... and put on the new [man], the man renewed in [or, to] knowledge according to the image of his Creator...

It is somewhat strange that Paul uses the word *neon* instead of the more usual *kainon* to designate the *new* man. *Neos* properly means a young man. Perhaps Paul was hinting that the Colossians were young, recently converted Christians. The meaning, however, is little different, for the context fixes the sense.

The remainder of the verse is of considerable importance for theology. In what sense is the Christian a new man? Why does Paul mention the image of the Creator? The Deity of Christ and his agency in creation were well motivated in 1:15 ff. But what in particular has creation now to do with ceasing to blaspheme and tell lies?

The first link of connection is the fact of regeneration. Regeneration is a second generation. It results in restoring to man, gradually, the original image of God that was defaced, defiled, deformed, depraved, though not destroyed. This verse fixes the chief characteristic of that image, namely, knowledge. In Ephesians 4:24 the new man is created in righteousness and holiness of truth. The text in Colossians does not deny that the image is characterized by righteousness and holiness. But it must be understood that righteousness is impossible without knowledge and truth. The nonrational animals cannot sin because they have no understanding. God imposed no moral laws on them. He gave them no verbal revelation. They and mankind are disparate species because man is God's image—a rational or knowing spirit.

Sin damaged man's mind. Sin did not invalidate the laws of logic, for these are the laws of God's own thought. Sin did not affect arithmetic. Two and two are still four; but on our check stubs we sometimes put three or five. The laws of thought are unaffected, but man as a sinner violates these laws. As with mistakes in arithmetic, so too men make mistakes in argumentation. They commit the fallacies of undistributed middle, the assertion of the consequent, and incomplete disjunction. Theology gives to such blunders the somewhat pedantic name of "noetic effects of sin." Let it also be noted that a logical blunder, wrong thinking, quickly and inevitably leads to overt sin. Before Eve and Adam bit into the apple, they had swallowed a bad thought.

Some exegetes reject the reference to God's original creation of Adam, and wish to restrict the meaning to his creation of the new man. The wording renders this impossible. The *ana* in *anakainoumenon* means "over again." Man is re-newed. But a re-newal presupposes a previous condition, and it is this previous condition to which "according to the image of the Creator" refers. The creation and the renewal are not the same event. The latter is possible only on the supposition of the former. God of course renews; God of course created. God created all; he renews only some. But these restrictions in no way remove from the verse the idea of the original creation. Man is renewed according to the original image, namely knowledge.

Now Paul urges the Colossians to avoid falsehood, on the ground that they are men renewed to knowledge and truth in accordance with the original image of their Creator.

3:11.   ... wherein (because of which circumstance) there is neither Greek nor Jew, circumcision or uncircumcision, Barbarian, Scythian, slave, freeman; but all things and in all things, Christ.

The Third Chapter of Colossians

The image of God, rationality, is the distinctive characteristic of the whole human race. Being Greek, Barbarian, or Scythian is not. The renewal of God's image eliminates these distinctions so far as the spiritual realm is concerned. In a narrower sphere circumcision and uncircumcision no longer count for anything. Social distinctions, slave and freeman, government official and private citizen, do not secure or bar entrance into the kingdom of heaven. All these distinctions are the result of sin. When Adam fell the unity of the human race was destroyed; or more accurately, when God shortly afterward regenerated them, he established the City of God, and Cain inherited and passed on the other city.

In another place, I Corinthians 3:28, Paul adds: "neither male nor female." This is somewhat different because the distinction between the sexes is not the result of sin. Their functions are different; but the spiritual level is the same. In the Old Testament their positions in worship were not the same; in the New Testament some ecclesiastical distinctions still remain; in heaven we shall be as the angels, neither marrying nor giving in marriage.

But as the prelapsarian distinction in sex remains, so too the postlapsarian distinctions of race and social position also remain. Paul did not free Onesimus from his servitude; the Zwickau prophets, John of Leyden, the Fifth Monarchy men, all perverted Christian political principles; and contemporary attempts to erase divine distinctions should also be opposed.

The word "wherein" or "under such conditions" may need a brief notice. Should this 'locality' or circumstance be identified as the new man, the knowledge, the image, or, hardly, the Creator? There is some reason to guess that the reference is to knowledge, because this knowledge includes the knowledge that these distinctions have no bearing on one's spiritual advancement. One might also suggest: "there where the image is found," or at least, "is found renewed." On the whole, however, it seems best not to select a single word or single factor as the antecedent of "wherein," but rather the whole of verse 10.

The final phrase of verse 11 is also more inclusive than distributive: "but all things and in all things Christ." The first *all* must be neuter; the second may be masculine, but not too plausibly so. The construction is concise. One cannot simply supply the verb *to be*, for it just is not true that Christ *is* all things: he is not a tree or a rock. Christ may be said to be in all things, or in all people, by reason of his creative power, and in all his people by reason of his recreative power. But in conformity with the preceding verses, it might be better to paraphrase it as: "social distinctions are unimportant and Christ is absolute in every respect."

> 3:12–14. Accordingly, as God's elect, holy and beloved, clothe yourselves with the compassion of mercy, generosity, humility, meekness, longsuffering, tolerating one another, and forgiving each other when anyone has a complaint against anyone; as even the Lord forgave you, so you also (should forgive). Above these, love, which is the bond of perfection.

The doctrine of election has not so far been mentioned in this context, unless one finds it implicit in the notion that God creates and recreates. A sinner willingly accepts Jesus as Lord because God had previously chosen him and made him willing. The depraved mind or will would never of itself make such a choice because the carnal mind is enmity against God, for it is not subject to the law of God, neither indeed can be.

Here *eklectoi* is the noun; *holy* and *beloved* are adjectives.

Because the Colossians and all other Christians are such, Paul exhorts them to be compassionate. The newly reconstructed nature of the elect contains all these virtues implicitly, but to actualize them in daily conduct requires attention and will power. This point supports the rejection of Alford's view of verse 1.

Pastors can preach sermons with good examples or horrible violations of these virtues. Such preaching is worthwhile for the purpose of reminding the people of their profession. The verses themselves need little exegesis or explanation. But the congregations need reminding.

One phrase, however, is not so immediately clear. Is love an extra addition to all these? How is it the bond of perfection?

The Third Chapter of Colossians

If love is simply one more virtue *in addition to* the others, it could hardly be a bond that united them. Therefore it may be best to translate *epi* as "*above* these," or "*on* these" superimpose love as the bond of perfection. May we not suggest that love is the bond of perfection or completeness in the sense that love is defined as the sum total of Christian virtue? Christian Science had and has a great deal to say about the love of God, a love that allows no room for a propitiatory sacrifice. Situation ethics, more recently, makes love cover, or rather, excuse a multitude of sins. It is a principle so vague that it commands nothing and forbids nothing. Many Christians who are basically evangelical also use the theme of love without having much of a clear idea of it. But the Scripture is not so vague. We perceive the love of God in Christ's propitiatory sacrifice (I John 3:16). Human religious love consists in obeying God's laws (Rom. 13:8,10). In this sense love is the bond of perfection. It is the systematic unity of all the virtues. Love *means* being compassionate, generous, forgiving, truthful, and observing all other divine laws.

> 3:15.   And let the peace of Christ rule in your hearts, to which also you were called in one body; and be thankful.

In this verse the peace of Christ is not the objective peace with God, established by Christ's propitiating God's wrath and putting an end to enmity, but clearly a subjective tranquillity in our own minds, a freedom from emotion, passion, anger, and wrath.

This tranquillity is to rule us. *Brabeuetō* is a strange verb here. One of its compounds occurred in 2:18. Its basic meaning is the giving of an award by an umpire to the winner of an athletic contest. The umpire decides or rules the game. But how can tranquillity or a calm mind be an umpire or award a prize? We do, however, say that calm rules or reigns, when it is undisturbed. Professor Moule, whom we have criticized even a bit sharply in the preceding, explains this verse very appropriately: "The peace which Christ brings (cf. John XIV, 27), that is the peace which is the result of obedience to him: obedience to the will of Christ is to be the 'umpire' in our hearts, settling conflicts of will and bringing co-ordination and direction to life."

This is the peace into which we were called. As in 3:12, so here the idea of election or calling is mentioned but not emphasized. Then comes the phrase "in one body." The one body is the body of Christ, the church, the *ecclēsia*, the "called out." It is not the peace that calls the Colossians *into* one body; it is their inclusion in the body which gave them the peace.

The verse ends with the command, Be thankful. The command ought not to have been necessary; but some people like to grumble, no matter what.

> **3:16. Let the word of Christ dwell in you richly in all wisdom, as you instruct and admonish [or, teaching and instructing] each other in psalms, hymns, spiritual songs, in grace, singing in your hearts to God.**

The phrase "The word of God" is familiar to all who read the Bible; but sometimes its full meaning is dimly apprehended. The Greek term *logos* can indeed mean a word, such as *cat*, or *desk*. It can also mean an explanation, a book, a mathematical ratio, a sentence, plus several other similar things. One must remind the emotional Christian who thinks intellectual theology useless and almost sinful, that pietism is not pure Christianity. The gospel is an intelligible message. It includes the doctrines—and *doctrine* is a good translation of *logos* also—of the Trinity, the eternal decree, unconditional election, irresistible grace, and the rest. Paul urges us to have a rich, abundant, extensive knowledge of the teachings of Christ. This is wisdom. Some editors put a comma after *richly*, and none after *wisdom*. Others do the reverse. It does not seem to make much difference in the sense here; though in 1:28 wisdom was connected with teaching.

It is also grammatically correct, but a little awkward, that the participles *teaching* and *admonishing* have the dative pronoun *you* for the antecedent. It may also seem strange that this instruction is given in psalms, hymns, and songs. But in an age without printing, and when many could not read, and before catechisms had been worked out, singing the words was a good method of learning. It still is.

The present writer's spiritual and physical ancestors, whom he indeed reveres, used this verse in their argument for restricting congregational singing to the Psalms of David. The three terms were supposed to be three divisions of Psalms. But these three titles seem to be insertions in the Septuagint without Hebrew evidence. However that may be, neither this passage nor the parallel in Ephesians speaks of formal congregational worship at all. They rather picture a daily occurrence, presumably at home, or in some cases in a workshop owned and operated by Christians. It is an unorganized and spontaneous worship. No doubt it carries implications relative to the assembly on the Lord's Day; but the Covenanters seem forced to prohibit hymns on a cotter's Saturday night. At the same time, singing hymns does not imply that the cheap catchy ditties of some modern evangelism, if it is evangelism at all, are superior to the Psalms of David. And a hymn book without a good proportion of Psalms is not fit for a church service.

3:17. And everything whatever you do in word or deed, (do) all in the name of Lord Jesus, giving thanks to God the Father through him.

The section from verse 12 to verse 17 is hortatory. The next six verses are also, but their instructions are more specific, whereas the present section is rather general. Verse 17 concludes these generalities; indeed it is the most general of all.

Greek style ordinarily puts the emphatic word at or near the beginning of a sentence. Here the emphasis falls on "everything whatever." The lesser generalities of verse 12 and the more specific duties of verses 18 ff. are all included in the word *pan* (all), and repeated for extra emphasis in *panta* (all, plural) in the next line. Paul allows no exception.

The Third Chapter of Colossians

One may ask, What does it mean precisely to do all things "in the name of the Lord Jesus"? Christians usually end their prayers with the phrase, "In Jesus' name, Amen"; though they may often have only vague ideas of why such a phrase is customary. To speak in Jesus' name, not merely when we pray but in every conversation—whatever you do in word—is to speak with Christ's sanction and approval, as Eadie so well remarks, and adds, "Still... a man is not to say, 'in Christ's name I buy this article or sell that one....' But the apostle means that such ought to be the habitual respect to Christ's authority...." Eadie further works out this theme in acceptable detail.

3:18, 19. Wives, be subject to your husbands, as is proper in the Lord. Husbands, love your wives and do not be irritable toward them.

Women's lib is anti-Christian because it has a wrong idea of woman's role and an equally wrong idea of man. Man was created first, and then woman was made from the man's side for the purpose of being a help-meet to him. This superiority and inferiority is not the result of sin, but was inherent in the original state of righteousness. Sin destroyed the harmony, but the deleterious effects of sin will not be canceled by ERA.

First of all, the subjection of the wife to her husband is a form of subjection appropriate to the Lord's criteria. The wife is not a slave. Nor has the husband any authority to impose sinful burdens upon her. On the contrary the husband must love his wife and not irritate her. The loving union is broken by adultery, and it is well to note that the Old Testament condemns both sinners, the man as well as the woman, to the same penalty, namely, capital punishment. The Old Testament also assigns to the faithful wife important functions in the household. Read Proverbs 31:10–31. Ephesians 5:25 commands husbands to love their wives as Christ loved the Church, to the extent of sacrificing his life for hers. A Christian home is a happy one; but can anyone imagine Bella Abzug enjoying marriage—or her husband?

122

The Third Chapter of Colossians

3:20,21. Children, obey your parents in all respects, for this is pleasing to the Lord. Fathers, do not anger your children, that they may not suffer depression.

When Paul tells children to obey their fathers in all respects, he clearly has in mind a Christian father. Fathers who teach crime, encourage licentiousness, or who are guilty of child abuse are not to be obeyed in every respect. Lightfoot could say, "The rule is stated absolutely because the exceptions are so few that they may be disregarded." But Lightfoot's vision was limited to late nineteenth-century England—an almost ideal age and place. With the late twentieth-century's permissiveness and the breakdown of the family engineered by liberal politicians, the exceptions are far more than Lightfoot could have imagined. Child pornography did not exist, homosexuality was suppressed, and crime was less violent than it is now. Of course there were crime, prostitution, and other sins in those days. But General Booth, "In Darkest England," faced a less hostile world than Anita Bryant and Phyllis Schlafly now do. The Lord protect Christian parents and their children.

3:22. Slaves, obey your masters in the flesh in every respect, not by eye-service as man-pleasers, but in simplicity of heart, fearing the Lord.

The Roman government was often harsh, and the slaves had few rights; yet the Roman form of slavery was not so bad as the chattel slavery in nineteenth-century America. The Old Testament also allowed slavery, but it was much less terrible than other forms, and provided automatically for freedom. But even the Roman slave, if a Christian, was to do his job honestly, thoroughly, sincerely, in fear of the Lord. How much more should the present-day assembly-line mechanic, the clerks and salespersons, the independent plumber and carpenter, do an honest day's work to please the Lord!

3:23, 24. Whatever you do, work out of your soul, as to the Lord, and not to men, knowing that from the

The Third Chapter of Colossians

Lord you will receive the reward of your inheritance.
Serve the Lord Christ.

The first of these verses repeats verse 17 and echoes an idea from verse 22, with a slight change in wording. Verse 24 adds an idea so far absent. The Christian does not serve the Lord for nothing. The Lord has promised him a reward and an inheritance. Kant theorized that motivation by reward made the best of conduct immoral. But this is not the Christian position.[1]

3:25. For the unjust man will receive back what he did unjustly, and there is no 'pull' (with God).

This somewhat slangy translation avoids a common misunderstanding of the more elegant phrase, "God is no respecter of persons." The latter gives the impression that God treats all persons alike. This is not true. God did not treat all animals alike: he gave big ears to the elephant and a long neck to the giraffe. Why should not God treat various men in various ways? He does. One must not translate the phrase as "There is no partiality with God." There is. He loved Jacob but hated Esau, even though Esau is often pictured as a more amiable character. The verse means that God is not motivated by a man's personal character or social standing. An example of "respect of persons" is found in seventeenth-century France. When crime was committed, the court wanted to know first of all what was the rank of the guilty party. A man of lower rank would be punished more severely than one of higher rank; and a still higher rank would excuse the criminal completely. Nobility had pull. There is no pull with God; he does not consider a man's person or position. If he pardons the guilty, as he does in the case of his elect, it is totally of grace, unmotivated by any merit in the sinner. But to say that God is impartial would mean that he pardons everyone. This is not what the Bible teaches.

1.Cf. my early article, "Kant and Old Testament Ethics," *The Evangelical Quarterly,* July 1935. London.

The Fourth Chapter

4:1.   Masters, grant justice and fairness to your slaves, knowing that you also have a master in heaven.

The word *masters* is the plural of *kurios*, the usual title given to Jesus: *Lord*. In verse 22 it occurred in the phrase "masters according to the flesh." England has a house of lords; and in modern Greek *kurios* means *monsieur*. Such is linguistic usage. The context determines what sort of lord, earthly or heavenly, is meant.

Another word, *isotēta*, does not mean equality in this instance, though a schoolboy would almost automatically so translate it. There were ranks among the slaves. They were not equal. But the master should treat them all fairly. Meyer, with some linguistic plausibility, wishes to take the word as *equality*. But since this idea does not fit the legal and social condition, he restricts it to equality in the spiritual realm. This had already been said in verse 11. But here verse 22 urges Christian slaves to obey even non-Christian masters so that the present verse must urge Christian masters not to mistreat even non-Christian slaves, . . . for they know that they too have a master in heaven.

The Fourth Chapter of Colossians

4:2. Persist in prayer, be alert in it in thanksgiving...

Bibles that try to outline the epistle by marking off paragraph divisions do different things at this point. One makes 3:18 a new paragraph with the head of "Social Duties in the New Life" and starts 4:2 with the title "Exhortations"; then 4:7 begins "Final Greetings." Another agrees with the divisions, but uses the headings, "Personal Relations in the New Life," "Instructions," and "Final Greetings." Still a third begins 3:5 with the heading "IV Exhortation," plus the subhead, "Put on Christ." Then there is no break until "Salutations" at 4:7. Near the beginning of this present study the difficulty in making an ideal outline was noted. There are indeed visible breaks, but sometimes Paul resumes a previous theme. And isn't a small division, like 4:2–6, only eight lines, with the heading "Exhortations," a little awkward?

Verse 2 urges the Colossians to pray persistently. They are to keep awake. This latter verb does not require midnight vigils in monasteries. It does not even mean, "Don't fall asleep on your knees." But rather, so it appears, it urges alertness to the needs of the time. One can pray in very general terms that apply to almost anything. This is sometimes very proper, so that the Anglican prayer book (mostly) is excellent for congregational prayer in all ages. But individual prayer, and even congregational prayer at times, can concern itself with particular matters. The church can always pray for "peace in our time;" but at a certain juncture it should pray, Restrain Hitler, or, Calm the Mid-East. In fact, the next verse indicates a particular petition for the Colossians, which we today cannot pray for concretely.

4:3. ... praying together [or, at the same time] also for us, that God may open to us a door for the word, to speak the mystery of Christ, because of which also I am in chains...

When Paul says "us," he must mean Timothy and Epaphras, but he hardly means them only. At least we note that he mentions several others in the final section. But he also means himself individually, for he changes the verb to the first person singular before the verse ends. Paul was in chains. His being in bonds does not refer to the fact that he was a bondslave of Christ. That condition never prevented him from preaching. Chains in a Roman prison did.

The phrase, "open a door for the word" is usually taken metaphorically: an opportunity to preach. But there may also be here a latent literal sense: the opening of the door of the prison so that Paul could walk out. Of course, he would walk out to preach.

4:4. ... in order that I may make it [the mystery] clear, as it is necessary for me to speak.

There are two and perhaps three purpose clauses interwoven in these two verses: the purpose of the prayer is to obtain Paul's release; the purpose of the release is Paul's speaking the mystery; and the purpose of speaking as it was necessary to speak was the proclamation, but especially the clarification of the mystery in the minds of the hearers.

At this point Moule writes, "It is a particularly pointed paradox to speak of *to musterion* in connection with *phaneroun* (verse 4), when the verb means (as it does here) a public manifestation." Does Moule mean that the Greek mysteries or secrets were revealed only privately to individuals in a ceremony of initiation? This may be his meaning, for he adds that the verb is suitable for private communication. But unless the term *musterion* regularly brought to mind the Greek mystery religions, there would be no paradox. Many people might simply think vaguely of some divine revelation, perhaps by Homer, and take the possibility of a public explanation as quite natural. The Jews would not have thought of Homer, but they would indeed have been willing to expound the Old Testament to any Gentile audience willing to listen.

Surely Paul sees no paradox in explaining God's secrets in public. God revealed the secrets so that at first the Jews and later all nations should understand them. Paul labors under the *necessity* of giving the explanation. This is how he *must* speak. Paradox? No; utter clarity.

**4:5.   Conduct yourselves in wisdom before those out-
side [the church], make the most of the present opportunity.**

The first half of the verse is clear enough; the second half is not a
literal translation at all. Literally it says something like "buying the
moment." This is not to be explained as motivated by a supposed
imminent return of Christ, as if *kairos* meant a very short time
before that event. Rather the shortness of the moment is that shortness that so often characterizes any opportunity. Tomorrow we remember what we should have said yesterday.

**4:6.   Let your reasoning be always with grace, sea-
soned with salt, [and?] know how you ought to answer
each and everyone.**

The term here translated "reasoning" is *logos*, the word. As indi-
cated previously *logos* means word, book, explanation, doctrine,
sentence, and much else. Since the end of the verse presents a
situation in which someone asks about his faith, questions that he
must answer, the English words *reasoning, answering,* or *argumentation* are good translations. Of course it cannot mean a word, like
rock or *triangle*. At least it must be a sentence.
The sentence or explanation must be given with grace. Not
graceful or elegant literary style, but with a godly spirit appropriate
to the total situation. The non-Christian, it is hoped, will find the
answer agreeable. Paul then adds, "seasoned with salt." In English
we have unfortunately a phrase, "salty language," which is decidedly
not the meaning here. Nor can the word mean "caustic," for the idea
of graciousness immediately precedes. It cannot even mean witty.
To suppose that this seasoned language preserves the questioner
from decay is too ingenious. Rather it is a quality that makes the
explanation interesting. Eggs without salt are insipid. We do not salt
them to preserve them, but to make them taste good. With this
example, we may suppose that Paul rejects vague, banal, meaning-

less phrases, and commends sharply defined terms to avoid misunderstanding so far as is possible. This correct and accurate kind of speech requires skill and knowledge. Hence Paul either commands us, "... know how you ought to speak," or perhaps, "... use grace and salt so that you will know." This latter, construing the verb as the infinitive of consequence, does not seem to make too good sense. Knowing how to speak is not the result of grace and salt; graciousness and salt are the result of knowing how to speak. Therefore, and it is grammatically admissible, it seems better to take the infinitive as an imperative idea.

That this kind of speech requires skill and knowledge, and not simply good intentions, is clear from the words "each and every" inquirer. Few people can answer each and every inquirer intelligently. Probably none of us can. But this is the ideal, and there is no excuse for satisfaction with incompetence. Every Christian has the obligation of studying the Bible assiduously, attentively, constantly, diligently, perseveringly, pertinaciously, seriously, strenuously, and any other adverbs that should stimulate the indolent.

> **4:7-9.** All my own affairs, Tychicus, the beloved brother, faithful servant (deacon) and co-bondsman in the Lord, will make known to you, whom I sent to you for this very purpose, that you might know our condition and that he might comfort your hearts, with Onesimus, the faithful and beloved brother, who is of you [r congregation]. They will inform you about everything here [in Rome].

There are only a few minor points that need explanation in this concluding section; and however difficult it may be to arrange a neat outline for the epistle, here is indeed the concluding section.

First, the word *diakonos*, applied to Tychicus, probably does not mean *deacon* in its official sense. In the New Testament the word bears its official meaning only infrequently. I Timothy 3:8, 12 are clear examples, but Phoebe in Romans 16:1 was a servant, not a deacon.

Second, there is a textual problem in verse eight. The Textus Receptus reads: "for this very purpose, that he may learn your circumstances and comfort your hearts." Now, it is within the range of possibility that the Colossians needed comfort because of some yet unknown trouble that Tychicus would learn of when he arrived. But this possibility does not fit well into the sentence as a whole. Paul sent Tychicus "for this very purpose," that is, to inform the Colossians of Paul's condition. The purpose is "that you Colossians may know"—not that Tychicus may know. Furthermore, though Tychicus is to comfort their hearts, this need not relate to Colossian troubles. They may have been quite upset about Paul, and Tychicus could comfort them on that score, for Paul might indeed yet be freed. In fact, he may have been. A third reason in favor of the reading of A, B, C, versus p46, Aleph 3, C, D3, and some cursives, is the repetition at the end of verse 9: they will inform you about everything here.

> **4:10,11.   Aristarchus, my fellow-prisoner, sends you his greetings, and Mark, the cousin of Barnabas, concerning whom you received instruction to receive him if he should come to you, and Jesus who is called Justus, these, being of the circumcision, are (my) only co-workers toward the kingdom of God, who have been a comfort to me.**

Although these verses, when read themselves, seem to say that of all Christians in Rome only these few Jewish Christians showed Paul any kindness, the context requires the interpretation that of all the Jewish Christians in Rome, only these showed him kindness. Luke was a Gentile (vs. 14 below).

Some commentators refuse to take "receive him" as the instructions mentioned in verse 10. But they have to acknowledge that no other instructions can be found. Further, since Paul and Mark had separated under unpleasant circumstances, it might have been wise for Paul to tell the Colossians to receive him. In any case the verse shows that the two had been reconciled.

4:12,13.   Epaphras, of your own [congregation], a slave of Christ, sends you greetings, always agonizing for you in his prayers that you may stand perfect and complete in every will of God, for I bear witness on his behalf that he is greatly afflicted over you, over those in Laodicea, and those in Hierapolis.

4:14, 15.   Luke, the beloved physician, and Demas greet you. You greet the brethren in Laodicea, and Nymphas with the church in his [or, her] house.

There is a divergence of opinion as to whether Nymphas was a man or woman, for some MSS have the masculine and others the feminine pronoun.

4:16   And when this epistle has been read before you, make [copies] that it may also be read in the Laodicean church, and the epistle from Laodicea that you also may read (it).

As the epistle approaches its last line, the wording becomes very concise. The meaning obviously is that the Laodiceans are to send to the Colossians a letter they have. This letter might be a now lost Pauline epistle. But not necessarily. If the epistle to the Ephesians be a circular letter, the Laodiceans may have had a copy that Paul here requests to be forwarded to Colosse. The text does not identify it as a letter *to* the Laodiceans, but a letter *from* Laodicea. This *from* can hardly be a letter from Laodicea to Paul, nor surely to Colosse; it is simply a letter that is now in Laodicea and should be sent from there to Colosse.

At any rate we can assume that the recipients of Paul's letters made copies and sent them to other congregations. Before the first century was three quarters gone, many congregations must have had several or many of the New Testament books, and the larger churches probably possessed the complete canon. In view of the poverty and low social status of the Christians, and because of harassment and persecution, it is unlikely that any copies were made on vellum. All would be papyri. When papyrus is buried in the sands of the Sahara, it lasts two thousand years. When it was handled every week, or every day, in winter as well as in summer, it wore out more rapidly, and new copies had to be made. In the fourth and fifth centuries when persecution had ceased, and before the barbarians destroyed the West, there were time and funds for using vellum. But by this time variant readings had already come into existence. There was much less alteration after A.D. 450 than before. Just because p46, p64, p66, and p67 date from the second century does not of itself prove that they are closer to the originals than some later cursive, or some later uncial. One must remember that very early heretics deliberately altered the text. The most serious alterations came early, not late. But here is not the place to pursue the tedious and intricate details of textual criticism. Those who wish to do so can find an abundant literature.

4:17.   And tell Archippus, See to the ministry (diaconate) which you received in the Lord, that you may fulfil it.

Here is a case where *diakonian* rather clearly indicates an ecclesiastical office. Archippus had received the office "in the Lord." He was to fulfil its obligations.

4:18.   The greeting of Paul in my own hand. Remember my chains. Grace be with you.

And the Textus Receptus adds (or does it preserve?),

Amen.

Appendix on Apokatēllagēte *in 1:22*

Though the details of textual criticism are often beyond the immediate concern of a commentary, as well as beyond the interest of many readers, yet this verse exemplifies difficulties which deserve mention somewhere. The appendix proposes to be the somewhere where some readers can find information not generally known. The matter at hand is not only a matter of textual criticism but also an account of how a group of editors finally published a critical text.

In this verse the Aland-Black-Metzger-Wikgren text prints *apokatēllagēte,* in the first and second (?) editions. The third edition has *apokatēllaxen.* Now, first, we shall consider the textual problem, and, second, the work of the editors.

The verb *apokatēllagēte* makes no sense. The only manuscript evidence cited in its support is B and papyrus 46. The other reading, which makes good sense, is supported by Aleph, A, C, D ^{c}, K, and many cursives. The textual problem therefore is settled by the manuscript evidence and by the argument in the commentary.

The work of the committee now presents an interesting phenomenon. In spite of the manuscript evidence and the exegetical argument in this commentary, the Aland text in its early editions printed the poorer reading. In the third edition the better reading appeared. After the publication of the third edition Professor Metzger published *A Textual Commentary on the Greek New Testament* in which

Appendix

the choices and decisions of the editors are explained. For this verse
two explanations are given. The first explanation, because its form
does not diverge from that of the other notes, seems to be the opinion of the majority of editors—a majority of three (or four?) to one.
The note reads:

> The conflicting textual phenomena of this verse are difficult to
> resolve. On the one hand, the reading apokatēllaxen is well
> supported (A C D^c K, nearly all minuscules: it 61, 68 vg syrP, ^{h}
> cop^{sa}, ^{bo}al) and provides acceptable sense. On the other hand,
> if this were the original reading, it is exceedingly difficult to
> explain why the other readings should have arisen. Faced with
> this dilemma, and considering a passive verb to be totally un-
> suitable in the context, a majority of the committee preferred
> to follow the proponderance of external testimony and there-
> fore adopted apokatēllaxen.

Since the majority decision did not control the published text of
the first edition, one seems forced to conclude that Professor Metzger alone decided what to print. In his *Textual Commentary*, after
recording the majority decision, he adds in brackets his own disagreement.

> [Despite the harsh anacoluthon that a passive verb creates af-
> ter umas in ver. 21, only apokatēllagēte, which is attested by
> diversified and early witnesses (B Hilary Ephraem, as well as,
> in effect, p^{46} and 33, both of which have scribal misspellings
> the presuppose -ēllagēte), can account for the rise of the other
> readings as more or less successful attempts to mend the syn-
> tax of the sentence. B.M.M.]

Now, quite aside from the question of how one vote carries over
three, the important point is how one evaluates variant readings.
The objective, textual evidence for the third singular active aorist,
which makes perfect sense and perfect grammar, is overwhelming.
Only two manuscripts are listed for the nonsense word. The majority of the editors accepted the objective evidence, even though they
acknowledge a subjective problem. Professor Metzger, who over-
rode them, bases his decision on subjective suppositions.

The problem is this: If the majority reading be the original, could a scribe have altered it into nonsense? And if the nonsense reading were original, would a scribe have corrected it? When so put, it is easy to say that a scribe could have corrected the nonsense word in order to give sense to the sentence. No one, I suppose, denies that possibility. But this is far from proving that such was the case. For one thing, it makes Paul write nonsense. Now, admittedly, the Lord did not give Paul the flair for delightful literary style. But scholar that he was, he did not make stupid grammatical blunders. It is much more likely that Paul expressed himself correctly in this verse.

In the second place, although sometimes there are very plausible assumptions as to what the copyists did, there are more cases otherwise. The case of the homoioteleuton is rather clear: either the copyist dropped a line, or he wrote the same line twice. But many more variants are due to carelessness. They are unintentional and inexplicable. Thus it is quite possible that a scribe with apokatēllaxen in front of his eyes might write apokatēllagēte. Stupid; but the present writer has also done some stupid things. Professor Metzger therefore depends solely on his own brilliance and disdains the objective evidence.

There is also another explanation of some variants, though it hardly applies in this case. Unlike the variants in secular manuscripts, such as Aristotle's *Physics* and Plato's *Timaeus,* all of which are unintentional blunders, the manuscripts of the New Testament were sometimes deliberately altered for theological reasons. Therefore we cannot treat the Bible just as we treat any other ancient book. Not only is there the vast quantitative difference between eight, 10, or 20 copies of Plato and four to five thousand copies of the New Testament; but there are these deliberate alterations also. No one can explain in detail the exceptional diversity of manuscript D. Maybe Aleph and B were deliberately altered. So far as I know there is no evidence to prove so; but there is evidence right before one's eyes, of several thousand differences between these two manuscripts, and presumably more between these two and a thousand cursives.

The knowledge that some heretics published altered texts invalidates the principle that the oldest manuscripts must be the best. This might be true if all errors were accidental. But the heretical changes were made early. It is at least possible that the heretical copyist used an original letter of Gospel. Hence it is not the fourth, fifth, or later centuries in which the defective manuscripts appear; it is the second century, or even the end of the first.

For these reasons, the subjective criteria used by a modern editor have little or no weight in comparison with the objective textual evidence.

To conclude and avoid misunderstanding, it is acknowledged that the third edition prints the better reading.

Index

Abel, 94, 95

Abraham, 41, 43, 46, 64, 73, 85, 94

Abzug, Bella, 122

Ad hominem arguments, 92

Adam, 28, 43, 46, 89, 115-118

Adoption, 38

Adultery, 122

Aland-Black-Metzger-Wikgren Text, 53, 61, 113, 133

Alford, H., *Works: Commentary on Colossians,* 24, 27, 61, 91, 96, 110-111, 118

American Standard Version, 29, 43, 57, 62

Anabasis (Xenophon), 106

Angels, 10, 36, 40-41, 52-53, 55, 58, 92, 98-102, 109-110, 117-118; worship of, 99, 109

Anger (of God), 113

Anselm, 60

Anthropocentric religion, 41-42

Anti-intellectualism, 67, 74

Antiquities (Josephus), 79

Apollos, 102

Apologetics, 23, 78

Apostleship, of Paul, 13

Aquinas, Thomas, 23

Archippus, 132

Ares, 41

Arianism, 34-39, 42

Aristarchus, 130

Aristophanes, *Works: The Clouds,* 9

Aristotle, 9, 17, 79, 102, 135; *Works: Physics,* 135

Arius, 34-39

Arminianism, 101

Arndt and Gingrich, 48

Asceticism, 8-9, 55, 103-108

Astrology, 9-10

Athanasius, 34-35, 71-72

Atheism, 74

Atonement, 51, 56

Attributes, of God, 80

Augustine, 20, 60, 72, 83, 94

Authorities, 39

Authority, 13

Authorship, of Colossians, 7

137

Index

Axioms, 79

Balaam, 41
Baptism, 84-87, 98, 102, 110-111
Baptismal regeneration, 86
Barnabas, 130
Barr, James, *Works: The
Semantics of Biblical
Language,* 19n.
Basilides, 8, 40, 80
Behaviorism, 33, 110
Believers, 15
Bellarmine, Robert, 59
Bible, 33, 84
Blood, 55
Bodies, 33, 107
Booth, General, 123
Bruce, F.F., *Works:
Commentary on the Epistle to
the Colossians,* 39, 111
Bryant, Anita, 123
Bultmann, Rudolph, 16, 66

Cain, 95-96, 118
Cajetan, 59
Calling, effectual, 77
Calvin, John, 23, 60, 67, 68, 72, 74,
81, 83, 90
Carson, Herbert M., *Works:
Colossians and Philemon,* 8-9,
25, 64, 71, 91, 97
Casuistry, 25
Celibacy, 103, 105
Ceremonial law, 90, 96
Cerinthus, 8
Chalcedonian Creed, 65, 66
Chemistry, 75
Cherubim, 41; *see also*

Angels
Christ, Jesus, 8; deity of, 34, 37,
43, 50, 166; person of, 48; pic-
tures of, 33; preeminence of,
49; pre-existence of, 43; return
of, 82; role of, 48; sacrifice of,
52; *see also* Christology *and*
Parousia
Christian Science, 119
Christmas, 94, 96, 104-105
Christology, 31-37, 45, 54, 65,
66, 73, 76, 77, 84, 85, 99, 101,
115; *see also* Christ
Chrysostom, 60, 67, 94
Church, 44-46, 47-49, 58-60, 62,
120, 122; calendar of, 94
Circumcision, 84-86, 98
City of God, 20, 117
Clark, Gordon H., *Works:*
"Kant and Old Testament
Ethics," 124; *The Philosophy of
Science,* 75
Clement, 99
Clergy, 14
Clouds, The (Aristophanes), 9
Colosse, 54
Colossians and Philemon
(Herbert M. Carson), 8-9, 25,
64, 71, 91, 97
*Commentary on the Epistle to
the Colossians* (F.F. Bruce), 39,
111
Communicatio idiomatum, 81, 82
Communion, 82
Construing a sentence, 11, 18, 28
Consubstantiation, 82
Conversion, 14
Corinth, 13, 55
Cosmic spirits, 79
Cosmos, 78-79

Index

Covenant, 84-85
Covenant of works, 89
Covenanters, 93, 96, 121
Creation, 38, 42, 48, 95, 116
Creator, 39, 46, 50
Creed of Chalcedon, 65-66
Cross, 50, 51, 55, 89-91
Crucifixion, of Christ, 32, 56, 92, 111
Curse, 52
Cynics, 9
Cyrenaics, 9

Daille, John, 70
Daniel, Bishop of Calcutta and Metropolitan of India, 71
David, 37, 41
Deity, of Christ, 34, 37, 43, 50, 166; *see also* Christ *and* Christology
Demas, 131
Democritus, 79, 82
Demons (devils), 10, 79, 92, 101-102, 110
Dewey, John, 33, 92
Diaconos, meaning of, 58, 61, 62, 129
Dialectical, 22
Dispersion, 99
Docetism, 55, 80
Doctrine, 67n.
Dominion, 36-37

Eadie, John, *Works: Commentary on Colossians*, 18, 26, 48, 60, 64, 72, 74, 87, 97, 108n., 114, 115, 122

Easter, 94, 96
Eden, 41
Egypt, 94
Elect, 46, 61, 118
Election, 11, 118, 120
Elements, 79, 102, 103
Emotion, 54-55, 74, 112-113, 119
Emotionalism, 22
Empedocles, 79
Empiricism, 92
Epaphras, 20-24, 67, 78, 126, 131
Ephesus, 69
Epicureans, 25, 40
Epistle to the Colossians, The (A.S. Peake), 24, 30
Epistles of Paul the Apostle to the Colossians and to Philemon, The (C.F.D. Moule), 32, 43-44, 60, 61, 70, 80, 81, 90, 91, 97, 102, 113, 115, 116, 119, 127
Equal Rights Amendment, 122
Erasmus, 55
Eriugena, John Scotus, 76
Esau, 85, 124
Essenes, 8, 9, 79
Eternal Generation, 38
Eternity, 42
Etymology, 24
Evangelical Quarterly, The, 124n.
Evangelistic endeavor, 16
Eve, 117
Exegesis, 11
Existence of God, 23
Existentialism, 78, 92
Exodus, 94

Index

Faith, 19, 20, 56, 57, 59, 63, 72, 77, 84, 87, 101
Fallacies, 75, 117
Feast of Tabernacles, 93
Feelings, 74
Feminism, 122
Fifth Monarchy men, 117
Firstborn, meaning of, 35-38
Flesh, meaning of, 88, 101, 106-108
Food laws, 92-93, 106
Forgiveness, 31
Freud, Sigmund, 10
Fuller, B.A.G., *Works: History of Greek Philosophy,* 52

Gabriel, 4, 41, 43
Galatia, 13
Galen, 102
Gentiles, 63-65, 73, 88
Gingrich and Arndt, 48
Glorification, 31
Glory 64, 65
Gnosticism 7-9, 10, 40-42, 49, 74, 80
God the Father, 13, 28, 34, 42, 47, 49, 50, 53, 61, 82-83, 110, 121
God the Son, 29, 42, 50, 82; *see also* Jesus Christ
God, 10, 80, 82; anger of, 113; existence of, 23; image of, 32, 48, 116, 118; whole counsel of, 24, 66; wrath of, 112-114
Good works, 26
Gospel, 16, 20, 21, 22, 29, 56-58, 64-66, 73, 74, 77, 97, 113
Grace, 16, 21-22, 120
Grammatical Insights into the New Testament (Nigel Turner), 9
Graven images, 33
Greek philosophy, 25
Greek Fathers, 81
Greek Orthodox, 97
Guilt, 16

Head, and heart, 54, 70
Heaven, 10, 110
Hegelianism, 78
Heidelberg Catechism, 66
Hell, 110
Hellenistic Judaism, 25
Hermes Trismegistus, 8
Hinduism, 20
Hippocrates, 102
History of Greek Philosophy, The (B.A.G. Fuller), 52
Hitler, Adolf, 126
Hodge, Charles, 34
Holy Spirit, 21, 22, 82, 110
Homer, 127
Homosexuality, 123
Hope, 20, 56
Humanism, 9, 92, 110
Humility, 8, 99, 107
Hymns, 120-121
Hypocrisy, 77

Icons, 33
Idolatry, 33, 41, 112
Image of God, 32, 33, 34, 115, 117
Immersion, 86-87
Imputation, 77
Incarnation, 33, 50, 84
Indulgences, 59
Inerrancy, of Bible, 66
Intellect, 54

Index

Interpretation, 11, 55, 106
Invisibility, God's, 33
Irenaeus, 89
Ishmael, 85
Islam, 83
Israel, 36, 37, 64

Jacob, 41, 124
James, William, 82
Jehovah, 8
Jehovah's Witnesses, 34, 35, 37, 76, 78
Jerusalem, 32
Jerusalem Bible, 57
Jesus, *see* Christ *and* God the Son
John, 25
John the Baptist, 37
John of Leyden, 117, 118
Josephus, *Works: Antiquities,* 79
Joy to the World, 52
Judaism, 25, 79
Judas Iscariot, 85
Justification, 77, 87
Justus, 130

Kairos, meaning of, 128
Kant, Immanuel, 100, 122, 124
"Kant and Old Testament Ethics," (Gordon H. Clark), 124
Kierkegaard, Soren, 54
King James Version, 43, 57, 62, 70, 77, 80, 97, 98, 99, 100, 103, 105, 106, 111, 123
Kingdom, 29, 30
Knowledge, 23-26, 27, 66-68, 72, 73, 74, 75, 80, 83, 115-117, 120, 128

Laban, 95
Laodiceans, 69, 70
Law, Ceremonial, 89
Law, Divine, 26, 27, 85, 90
Law of contradiction, 82
Lazarus, 37
Legalism, 27
Licentiousness, 9, 55
Liddell and Scott, 91
Lie, 114
Life after death, 10
Lightfoot, J.B., *Works: Saint Paul's Epistles to the Colossians and to Philemon,* 7, 8, 9, 72, 73, 75, 90, 91, 96, 100, 102, 103, 111, 113, 123
Logic, 75, 78, 82, 92, 116, 117
Logical Positivism, 33, 78, 110
Logos, 10, 39, 42, 120, 128
Lombard, Peter, 26
Lord's Supper, 85, 98
Lot, 41
Love, 20, 22, 119
Luke, 130-131
Luther, Martin, 55, 60, 62
Lyceum, 9
Lystra, 69

Mariolatry, 99, 117
Mark, 130
Marriage, 94, 103, 117, 118
Mary, 35, 36, 43, 101
Masters, and slaves, 125
Materialism, 78
Matter, 8
Mediator, 99

Index

Memorabilia (Xenophon), 106
Metzger, Bruce, *Works: A Textual Commentary on the Greek New Testament,* 53, 97, 113, 133-134
Meyer, F.B., *Works: Commentary on Colossians,* 38, 39, 47, 48, 49, 50, 59, 69, 70, 88, 91n., 97, 101, 125
Michael (archangel), 41, 43, 100
Middle Ages, 89, 100
Midrash, 25
Millennium, 30, 97
Mind, 70
Moral law, 90, 96; *see also* Law, Divine
Morality, 25
Mosaic law, 89, 90, 93
Moses, 19, 43, 46, 73, 95, 97, 99
Mother of God, 36
Moule, C.F.D., *Works: The Epistles of Paul the Apostle to the Colossians and to Philemon,* 32, 43-44, 60, 61, 70, 80, 81, 90, 91, 97, 102, 113, 115, 116, 119, 127
Mystery, 63-65, 72-73, 126-127
Mysticism, 76

Nagel, Ernest, 33
Nash, Ronald, 81
Naturalism, 33
Nature, 52, 78
Neo-orthodox, 22, 54
Neoplatonists, 9, 100
New American Standard, 21, 28, 29, 57, 105
New International Version, 106, 107

Nicene Creed, 66
Noah, 94
Noetic effects of sin, 116
Nymphas, 131

Object of belief, 15
Old Testament, 34
Olympics, 9
Omnipotence, of God, 38, 80, 81
Omnipresence, of God, 81
Omniscience, of God, 81
One-and-Many problem, 82
Onesimus, 117-118, 129
Ordaining women, 58
Origen, 99
Orthodoxy, 25
Ostervald, 62

Paley, William, 23
Parmenides, 82
Parousia, 47, 88, 112
Passover, 36, 93, 98
Paul, 7, 8, 9, 13, 24, 46; apostleship of, 13
Peace, 16, 50-51
Peake, A.S., *Works: The Epistle to the Colossians,* 24, 30
Pentecost, 93-94, 107
Permissiveness, 123
Pharaoh, 37
Pharisees, 19, 54, 79, 93
Philip, 34
Philo, 25, 39, 81
Philosophy, 74, 77-79
Philosophy of Science and Belief in God, The (Gordon H. Clark), 75
Phoebe, 58, 129

Index

Physics, 75
Physics (Aristotle), 135
Pietism, 12, 16, 22, 54, 74, 75, 120
Plato, 9, 17, 48, 79, 82, 102, 135; *Works: Timaeus,* 135
Pleroma, meaning of, 49, 50, 80, 83
Plotinus, 82
Poimander (Hermes Trismegistus), 8
Politics, 110
Pontifex maximus, 14
Pornography, 123
Poseidon, 41
Positivism, 33, 92, 110
Postlapsarianism, 117
Pragmatism, 92
Prayer, 30, 126
Pre-existence, of Christ, 43, 67
Predestination, 36, 60, 62, 64, 67
Prelapsarianism, 117
Presuppositions, 79
Pride, 77, 106
Principles, moral and religious, 103
Proclus, 100
Proofs, of God, 23
Propitiation, 56, 60-61
Protagoras, 92
Purgatory, 5, 59
Puritan principle, 96
Puritans, 22, 93, 96
Purpose of writing commentary, 7, 67n.
Pythagoreans, 63

Ransom, 30-31
Rationality, 117

Reason, 55
Reconciliation, 50-53, 56
Redemption, 8, 30-31, 50
Reformation, 53, 64, 67, 74
Reformed Presbyterian Church Evangelical Synod, 94
Regeneration, 84, 86, 87-88, 90, 115-116
Reitzenstein, R., 8
Renan, Ernst, 66
Resurrection, 46-48, 49, 57, 65, 66, 86, 88, 94
Revised Standard Version, 43, 57, 62, 105, 106
Romanism, 15, 59, 60, 97
Ryle, Gilbert, 10

Sabbath (Lord's Day), 92-96
Sacramentarianism, 14, 82
Sadducees, 19, 79, 93
Saint Paul's Epistles to the Colossians and to Philemon (J.B. Lightfoot), 7, 8, 9, 72, 73, 75, 90, 91, 96, 100, 102, 103, 111, 113, 123
Saints, 14, 15, 99, 105
Salvation, universal, 52
Sanctification, 31
Satan, 40-41, 91-92, 100
Schiller, F.C.S., 66, 92
Schlafly, Phyllis, 123
Schleiermacher, Friedrich, 52, 60
Schweitzer, Albert, 66
Science, 23, 74
Scientism, 74
Scofield Bible, 63
Secular learning, 26
Secularism, 10, 33, 41, 43
Self-existence, 80

143

Index

Semantics of Biblical Language, The (James Barr), 19n.

Sensation, 23, 34, 92

Septuagint, 76, 121

Servetus, 74

Simon Magus, 8

Sin, 30-31, 50, 90

Situation ethics, 119

Skinner, B.F., 10

Slavery, 123, 125

Socinus, 74

Sodom, 41

Sola Scriptura, 63

Sophia, 40

Sovereignty, of God, 80

Spirits, 103

Spirituality, 16

Stephen, 99

Stoa, 9

Stoics, 25, 40

Strauss, David F., 66

Style, Paul's, 18, 126

Suarez, Francisco, 59

Subjectivism, 16

Suffering, 58-60

Talmud, 25

Ten Commandments, 26, 90, 95-97

Tertullian, 78, 113

Textual Commentary on the Greek New Testament, A (Bruce Metzger), 53, 97, 113, 133-134

Textual criticism, 11, 16-17, 130-136

Textus Receptus, 130, 132

Thanksgiving, 76, 77

Thayer's *Lexicon,* 31

Theocentric religion, 41, 42

Theodoret, 99

Theology, 27, 66

Thrones, meaning of, 40

Timaeus, (Plato), 135

Timothy, 13-14, 17, 126

Tischendorf, 113

Titus, 13

Torrance, Thomas, 19n.

Tradition, 77, 79, 80

Transubstantiation, 82

Treasury of the saints, 59

Trinity, 27, 82-83, 92, 110, 120

Trismegistus, Hermes, *Works: Poimander,* 8

Truth, 20, 21, 25, 29, 74, 77, 92, 116

Turner, Nigel, *Works: Grammatical Insights into the New Testament,* 9

Tychicus, 127, 129, 130

Uncircumcision, 88

Understanding, 25-27, 72; *see also* Knowledge

Unitarians, 74

Universal brotherhood of man, 20

Universal fatherhood of God, 20

Valentinus, 8, 40, 80

Warfield, B.B., 34

Wealth, 64, 71-73

Westminster Confession, 63, 66

Westminster Shorter Catechism, 30, 63, 66, 90, 96

Index

When Peace Like a River, 90
Will, 70; of God, 6, 24, 25
Wisdom, 23, 25-27, 66, 72-75, 83
Word of God, 62, 66, 120
World War II, 42

Xenophon, *Works: Anabasis,*
  Memorabilia, 106

Zanchius, Jerome, 60
Zeus, 41
Zwickau prophets, 117

Scripture Index

Acts
6:1ff. *58*
6:6 *58*
10 *90*
17:18 *25, 40*
17:22 *13*
20:20-31 *67n.*
20:27 *24*

I Corinthians *14, 88, 104*
1:21 *49*
1:30 *67n.*
2:6, 7 *67n.*
2:16 *54, 67n.*
3:2 *25, 67n.*
3:9 *76*
3:28 *117*
6:13 *104*
8:4 *41*
9:27 *107*
10:20 *41*
11:7 *33*
12:12-14, 27 *102*
12:21 *45*

13:8-10 *119*
15:24, 28 *53*
15:51 *63, 64*

II Corinthians *14*
1:12 *104, 106*
4:4 *32*

Deuteronomy
10:16 *85*
30:6 *85*

Ephesians
1:10 *53*
1:13 *20*
1:22-23 *4*
2 *64*
2:3 *96*
2:8 *101*
2:12 *54*
3 *64*
3:5 *63*
4:14-15 *102*
4:24 *115*

5:25 *122*
12:21 *45*

Exodus
4:22 *36*
16 *95*
16:23, 25-26 *95*
20 *95*

Galatians *104*
2:11ff. *90*
2:19-20 *111*
5:19-21 *55*

Genesis
1 *44*
2:3 *94-96*
3:17-18 *52*
7:4, 10 *95*
8:10, 12 *95*
12:3 *85*
17:2 *85*
17:10 *85*
17:12 *95*
18 *41*
21:4 *95*
29:27-28 *95*
47:1 *94*

Hebrews
1:6 *36*
5:12, 13 *25*
6:1-2 *67n.*
11:28 *36*
12:23 *36*
13:13 *61*

John *67n.*
1:1 *37*
1:15 *37*

5:46-47 *19*
14:15 *90*
14:27 *119*

I John
3:1-2 *112*
3:16 *119*

Judges
6 *41*

Leviticus
23 *93*

Luke
1:2 *49*
2:7 *36*
6:36 *49*

Mark
9:50 *48, 49*

Matthew
4:6 *41*
4:17 *63*
8:10 *19*
9:2, 22 *19*
9:28-29 *19*
10:16 *48*
12:1 *94*
16:28 *19*
20:23 *61*
20:25 *62*
21:21 *19*
23:23 *19*
23:32 *60*
28:1 *94*

Numbers
22 *41*

33:52   *33*

I Peter
  1:12   *53*
  4:13   *61*

II Peter   *7*
  3:10   *51*

Philippians
  2:12   *110*

Proverbs
  31:10-31   *122*

Psalms
  89:27   *37*
  91:11   *41*
  121   *41, 42*
  122   *41, 42*

Revelation
  19:10   *99*

Romans   *22, 104*
  1:1   *14*
  1:7   *15*
  1:14   *67n.*
  1:18   *113*

1:18, 21, 25   *54*
1:20   *80*
1:28   *54*
2:1   *13*
5:10   *54*
5:12-21   *115*
6   *26*
6:5   *86*
7   *26*
8   *26*
8:22   *51*
8:29   *36*
13:1   *39*
13:8, 10   *119*
16:1   *58, 129*

I Thessalonians
  2:16   *60*

I Timothy   *13, 14*
  3:2   *67n.*
  3:8, 12   *129*

II Timothy   *13, 14*
  2:24   *67n.*
  4:2   *67n.*

Titus   *13*
  1:9   *67n.*

The Crisis of Our Time

Historians have christened the thirteenth century the Age of Faith and termed the eighteenth century the Age of Reason. The twentieth century has been called many things: the Atomic Age, the Age of Inflation, the Age of the Tyrant, the Age of Aquarius. But it deserves one name more than the others: the Age of Irrationalism. Contemporary secular intellectuals are anti-intellectual. Contemporary philosophers are anti-philosophy. Contemporary theologians are anti-theology.

In past centuries secular philosophers have generally believed that knowledge is possible to man. Consequently they expended a great deal of thought and effort trying to justify knowledge. In the twentieth century, however, the optimism of the secular philosophers has all but disappeared. They despair of knowledge.

Like their secular counterparts, the great theologians and doctors of the church taught that knowledge is possible to man. Yet the theologians of the twentieth century have repudiated that belief. They also despair of knowledge. This radical skepticism has filtered down from the philosophers and theologians and penetrated our entire culture, from television to music to literature. *The Christian in the twentieth century is confronted with an overwhelming cultural consensus—sometimes stated explicitly, but most often implicitly:*

151

The Crisis of Our Time

Man does not and cannot know anything truly.

What does this have to do with Christianity? Simply this: If man can know nothing truly, man can truly know nothing. We cannot know that the Bible is the Word of God, that Christ died for sin, or that Christ is alive today at the right hand of the Father. Unless knowledge is possible, Christianity is nonsensical, for it claims to be knowledge. What is at stake in the twentieth century is not simply a single doctrine, such as the Virgin Birth, or the existence of hell, as important as those doctrines may be, but the whole of Christianity itself. If knowledge is not possible to man, it is worse than silly to argue points of doctrine—it is insane.

The irrationalism of the present age is so thorough-going and pervasive that even the Remnant—the segment of the professing church that remains faithful—has accepted much of it, frequently without even being aware of what it was accepting. In some circles this irrationalism has become synonymous with piety and humility, and those who oppose it are denounced as rationalists—as though to be logical were a sin. Our contemporary anti-theologians make a contradiction and call it a Mystery. The faithful ask for truth and are given Paradox. If any balk at swallowing the absurdities of the anti-theologians, they are frequently marked as heretics or schismatics who seek to act independently of God.

There is no greater threat facing the true Church of Christ at this moment than the irrationalism that now controls our entire culture. Communism, guilty of tens of millions of murders, including those of millions of Christians, is to be feared, but not nearly so much as the idea that we do not and cannot know the truth. Hedonism, the popular philosophy of America, is not to be feared so much as the belief that logic—that "mere human logic," to use the religious irrationalists' own phrase—is futile. The attacks on truth, on revelation, on the intellect, and on logic are renewed daily. But note well: The misologists—the haters of logic—use logic to demonstrate the futility of using logic. The anti-intellectuals construct intricate intellectual arguments to prove the insufficiency of the intellect. The anti-theologians use the revealed Word of God to show that there can be no revealed Word of God—or that if there could, it would remain impenetrable darkness and Mystery to our finite minds.

The Crisis of Our Time

Nonsense Has Come

Is it any wonder that the world is grasping at straws—the straws of experientialism, mysticism and drugs? After all, if people are told that the Bible contains insoluble mysteries, then is not a flight into mysticism to be expected? On what grounds can it be condemned? Certainly not on logical grounds or Biblical grounds, if logic is futile and the Bible unintelligible. Moreover, if it cannot be condemned on logical or Biblical grounds, it cannot be condemned at all. If people are going to have a religion of the mysterious, they will not adopt Christianity: They will have a genuine mystery religion. "Those who call for Nonsense," C.S. Lewis once wrote, "will find that it comes." And that is precisely what has happened. The popularity of Eastern mysticism, of drugs, and of religious experience is the logical consequence of the irrationalism of the twentieth century. There can and will be no Christian revival—and no reconstruction of society— unless and until the irrationalism of the age is totally repudiated by Christians.

The Church Defenseless

Yet how shall they do it? The spokesmen for Christianity have been fatally infected with irrationalism. The seminaries, which annually train thousands of men to teach millions of Christians, are the finishing schools of irrationalism, completing the job begun by the government schools and colleges. Some of the pulpits of the most conservative churches (we are not speaking of the apostate churches) are occupied by graduates of the anti-theological schools. These products of modern anti-theological education, when asked to give a reason for the hope that is in them, can generally respond with only the intellectual analogue of a shrug—a mumble about Mystery. They have not grasped—and therefore cannot teach those for whom they are responsible—the first truth: "And ye shall know the truth." Many, in fact, explicitly deny it, saying that, at best, we possess only "pointers" to the truth, or something "similar" to the truth, a mere analogy. Is the impotence of the Christian Church a puzzle? Is the fascination with pentecostalism and faith healing among members of conservative churches an enigma? Not when one understands the sort of studied nonsense that is purveyed in the name of God in the seminaries.

The Trinity Foundation

The creators of The Trinity Foundation firmly believe that theology is too important to be left to the licensed theologians—the graduates of the schools of theology. They have created The Trinity Foundation for the express purpose of teaching the faithful all that the Scriptures contain— not warmed over, baptized, secular philosophies. Each member of the board of directors of The Trinity Foundation has signed this oath: "I believe that the Bible alone and the Bible in its entirety is the Word of God and, therefore, inerrant in the autographs. I believe that the system of truth presented in the Bible is best summarized in the Westminster Confession of Faith. So help me God."

The ministry of The Trinity Foundation is the presentation of the system of truth taught in Scripture as clearly and as completely as possible. We do not regard obscurity as a virtue, nor confusion as a sign of spirituality. Confusion, like all error, is sin, and teaching that confusion is all that Christians can hope for is doubly sin.

The presentation of the truth of Scripture necessarily involves the rejection of error. The Foundation has exposed and will continue to expose the irrationalism of the twentieth century, whether its current spokesman be an existentialist philosopher or a professed Reformed theologian. We oppose anti-intellectualism, whether it be espoused by a neo-orthodox theologian or a fundamentalist evangelist. We reject misology, whether it be on the lips of a neo-evangelical or those of a Roman Catholic charismatic. To each error we bring the brilliant light of Scripture, proving all things, and holding fast to that which is true.

The Primacy of Theory

The ministry of The Trinity Foundation is not a "practical" ministry. If you are a pastor, we will not enlighten you on how to organize an ecumenical prayer meeting in your community or how to double church attendance in a year. If you are a homemaker, you will have to read elsewhere to find out how to become a total woman. If you are a businessman, we will not tell you how to develop a social conscience. The professing church is drowning in such "practical" advice.

The Trinity Foundation is unapologetically theoretical in its outlook, believing that theory without practice is dead, and that practice without theory is blind. The trouble with the professing church is not primarily in its practice, but in its theory. Christians do not know, and many do not even care to know, the doctrines of Scripture. Doctrine is intellectual, and Christians are generally anti-intellectual. Doctrine is ivory tower philosophy, and they scorn ivory towers. The ivory tower, however, is the control tower of a civilization. It is a fundamental, theoretical mistake of the practical men to think that they can be merely practical, for practice is always the practice of some theory. The relationship between theory and practice is the relationship between cause and effect. If a person believes correct theory, his practice will tend to be correct. The practice of contemporary Christians is immoral because it is the practice of false theories. It is a major theoretical mistake of the practical men to think that they can ignore the ivory towers of the philosophers and theologians as irrelevant to their lives. Every action that the "practical" men take is governed by the thinking that has occurred in some ivory tower—whether that tower be the British Museum, the Academy, a home in Basel, Switzerland, or a tent in Israel.

In Understanding Be Men

It is the first duty of the Christian to understand correct theory—correct doctrine—and thereby implement correct practice. This order—first theory, then practice—is both logical and Biblical. It is, for example, exhibited in Paul's epistle to the Romans, in which he spends the first eleven chapters expounding theory and the last five discussing practice. The contemporary teachers of Christians have not only reversed the order, they have inverted the Pauline emphasis on theory and practice. The virtually complete failure of the teachers of the professing church to instruct the faithful in correct doctrine is the cause of the misconduct and cultural impotence of Christians. The Church's lack of power is the result of its lack of truth. The *Gospel* is the power of God, not religious experience or personal relationship. The Church has no power because it has abandoned the Gospel, the good news, for a religion of experientialism. Twentieth century American Christians are children carried about by every wind of doctrine, not knowing what they believe, or even if they believe anything for certain.

The chief purpose of The Trinity Foundation is to counteract the irrationalism of the age and to expose the errors of the teachers of the church. Our emphasis—on the Bible as the sole source of truth, on the primacy of the intellect, on the supreme importance of correct doctrine, and on the necessity for systematic and logical thinking—is almost unique in Christendom. To the extent that the church survives —and she will survive and flourish—it will be because of her increasing acceptance of these basic ideas and their logical implications.

We believe that the Trinity Foundation is filling a vacuum in Christendom. We are saying that Christianity is intellectually defensible—that, in fact, it is the only intellectually defensible system of thought. We are saying that God has made the wisdom of this world —whether that wisdom be called science, religion, philosophy, or common sense—foolishness. We are appealing to all Christians who have not conceded defeat in the intellectual battle with the world to join us in our efforts to raise a standard to which all men of sound mind can repair.

The love of truth, of God's Word, has all but disappeared in our time. We are committed to and pray for a great instauration. But though we may not see this reformation of Christendom in our lifetimes, we believe it is our duty to present the whole counsel of God because Christ has commanded it. The results of our teaching are in God's hands, not ours. Whatever those results, His Word is never taught in vain, but always accomplishes the result that He intended it to accomplish. Professor Gordon H. Clark has stated our view well:

The Crisis of Our Time

There have been times in the history of God's people, for example, in the days of Jeremiah, when refreshing grace and widespread revival were not to be expected: the time was one of chastisement. If this twentieth century is of a similar nature, individual Christians here and there can find comfort and strength in a study of God's Word. But if God has decreed happier days for us and if we may expect a world-shaking and genuine spiritual awakening, then it is the author's belief that a zeal for souls, however necessary, is not the sufficient condition. Have there not been devout saints in every age, numerous enough to carry on a revival? Twelve such persons are plenty. What distinguishes the arid ages from the period of the Reformation, when nations were moved as they had not been since Paul preached in Ephesus, Corinth, and Rome, is the latter's fullness of knowledge of God's Word. To echo an early Reformation thought, when the ploughman and the garage attendant know the Bible as well as the theologian does, and know it better than some contemporary theologians, then the desired awakening shall have already occurred.

In addition to publishing books, of which *Colossians* is the twenty-fifth, the Foundation publishes a bimonthly newsletter, *The Trinity Review*. Subscriptions to *The Review* are free; please write to the address below to become a subscriber. If you would like further information or would like to join us in our work, please let us know.

The Trinity Foundation is a non-profit foundation tax-exempt under section 501 (c)(3) of the Internal Revenue Code of 1954. You can help us disseminate the Word of God through your tax-deductible contributions to the Foundation.

And we know that the Son of God is come, and hath given us an understanding, that we may know him that is true, and we are in him that is true, in his Son Jesus Christ. This is the true God, and eternal life.

John W. Robbins
President

Intellectual Ammunition

The Trinity Foundation is committed to the reconstruction of philosophy and theology along Biblical lines. We regard God's command to bring all our thoughts into conformity with Christ very seriously, and the books listed below are designed to accomplish that goal. They are written with two subordinate purposes: (1) to demolish all secular claims to knowledge; and (2) to build a system of truth based upon the Bible alone.

Works of Philosophy

Answer to Ayn Rand, John W. Robbins $4.95
The only analysis and criticism of the views of novelist-philosopher Ayn Rand from a consistently Christian perspective.

Behaviorism and Christianity, Gordon H. Clark $5.95
Behaviorism *is a critique of both secular and religious behaviorists. It includes chapters on John Watson, Edgar S. Singer Jr., Gilbert Ryle, B.F. Skinner, and Donald MacKay. Clark's refutation of behaviorism and his argument for a Christian doctrine of man are unanswerable.*

Intellectual Ammunition

A Christian Philosophy of Education, Gordon H. Clark $8.95

The first edition of this book was published in 1946. It sparked the contemporary interest in Christian schools. Dr. Clark has thoroughly revised and updated it, and it is needed now more than ever. Its chapters include: The Need for a World-View, The Christian World-View, The Alternative to Christian Theism, Neutrality, Ethics, The Christian Philosophy of Education, Academic Matters, Kindergarten to University. Three appendices are included as well: The Relationship of Public Education to Christianity, A Protestant World-View, and Art and the Gospel..

A Christian View of Men and Things, Gordon H. Clark $8.95

No other book achieves what A Christian View *does: the presentation of Christianity as it applies to history, politics, ethics, science, religion, and epistemology. Clark's command of both worldly philosophy and Scripture is evident on every page, and the result is a breathtaking and invigorating challenge to the wisdom of this world.*

Clark Speaks From The Grave, Gordon H. Clark $3.95

Dr. Clark chides some of his critics for their failure to defend Christianity competently. Clark Speaks *is a stimulating and illuminating discussion of the errors of contemporary apologists.*

Education, Christianity, and the State $7.95
J. Gresham Machen

Machen was one of the foremost educators, theologians, and defenders of Christianity in the twentieth century. The author of numerous scholarly books, Machen saw clearly that if Christianity is to survive and flourish, a system of Christian grade schools must be established. This collection of essays captures his thought on education over nearly three decades.

Logic, Gordon H. Clark $8.95

Written as a textbook for Christian schools, Logic *is another unique book from Clark's pen. His presentation of the laws of thought, which must be followed if Scripture is to be understood correctly, and which are found in Scripture itself, is both clear and thorough.* Logic *is an indispensable book for the thinking Christian.*

The Philosophy of Science and Belief in God $5.95
Gordon H. Clark

In opposing the contemporary idolatry of science, Clark analyzes three major aspects of science: the problem of motion, Newtonian science, and modern theories of physics. His conclusion is that science, while it may be useful, is always false; and he demonstrates its falsity in numerous ways. Since science is always false, it can offer no objection to the Bible and Christianity.

Religion, Reason and Revelation, Gordon H. Clark $7.95
One of Clark's apologetical masterpieces, Religion, Reason and Revelation *has been praised for the clarity of its thought and language. It includes chapters on Is Christianity a Religion? Faith and Reason, Inspiration and Language, Revelation and Morality, and God and Evil. It is must reading for all serious Christians.*

Selections from Hellenistic Philosophy, Gordon H. Clark $10.95
This is one of Clark's early works in which he translates, edits, and comments upon works by the Epicureans, the Stoics, Plutarch, Philo Judaeus, Hermes Trismegistus, and Plotinus. First published in 1940, it has been a standard college text for more than four decades.

Three Types of Religious Philosophy, Gordon H. Clark $6.95
In this handbook on apologetics, Clark examines empiricism, rationalism, dogmatism, and contemporary irrationalism, which does not rise to the level of philosophy. He offers a solution to the question, "How can Christianity be defended before the world?"

William James, Gordon H. Clark $2.00
America has not produced many philosophers, but William James has been extremely influential. Clark examines his philosophy of Pragmatism.

Works of Theology

The Atonement, Gordon H. Clark $8.95
   This is a major addition to Clark's multi-volume systematic theology. In The Atonement, *Clark discusses the Covenants, the Virgin Birth and Incarnation, federal headship and representation, the relationship between God's sovereignty and justice, and much more. He analyzes traditional views of the Atonement and criticizes them in the light of Scripture alone.*

The Biblical Doctrine of Man, Gordon H. Clark $5.95
   Is man soul and body or soul, spirit, and body? What is the image of God? Is Adam's sin imputed to his children? Is evolution true? Are men totally depraved? What is the heart? These are some to the questions discussed and answered from Scripture in this book.

Cornelius Van Til: The Man and The Myth $2.45
John W. Robbins
   The actual teachings of this eminent Philadelphia theologian have been obscured by the myths that surround him. This book penetrates those myths and criticizes Van Til's surprisingly unorthodox views of God and the Bible.

Faith and Saving Faith, Gordon H. Clark $5.95
   The views of the Roman Catholic church, John Calvin, Thomas Manton, John Owen, Charles Hodge, and B.B. Warfield are discussed in this book. Is the object of faith a person or a proposition? Is faith more than belief? Is belief more than thinking with assent, as Augustine said? In a world chaotic with differing views of faith, Clark clearly explains the Biblical view of faith and saving faith.

God's Hammer: The Bible and Its Critics, Gordon H.
Clark $6.95
   The starting point of Christianity, the doctrine on which all other doctrines depend, is "The Bible alone is the Word of God written,

and therefore inerrant in the autographs." Over the centuries the opponents of Christianity, with Satanic shrewdness, have concentrated their attacks on the truthfulness and completeness of the Bible. In the twentieth century the attack is not so much in the fields of history and archaeology as in philosophy. Clark's brilliant defense of the complete truthfulness of the Bible is captured in this collection of eleven major essays.

The Incarnation, Gordon H. Clark $8.95
   Who was Christ? The attack on the Incarnation in the nineteenth and twentieth centuries has been vigorous, but the orthodox response has been lame. Clark reconstructs the doctrine of the Incarnation building and improving upon the Chalcedonian definition.

In Defense of Theology, Gordon H. Clark $12.95
   There are four groups to whom Clark addresses this book: the average Christians who are uninterested in theology, the atheists and agnostics, the religious experientialists, and the serious Christians. The vindication of the knowledge of God against the objections of three of these groups is the first step in theology.

Logical Criticisms of Textual Criticism, Gordon H. Clark $2.95
   In this critique of the science of textual criticism, Dr. Clark exposes the fallacious argumentation of the modern textual critics and defends the view that the early Christians knew better than the modern critics which manuscripts of the New Testament were more accurate.

Pat Robertson: A Warning to America, John W. Robbins $6.95
   The Protestant Reformation was based on the Biblical principle that the Bible is the only revelation from God, yet a growing political-religious movement, led by Pat Robertson, asserts that God speaks to them directly. This book addresses the serious issue of religious fanaticism in America by examining the theological and political views of Pat Robertson.

Predestination, Gordon H. Clark $7.95
   Clark thoroughly discusses one of the most controversial and pervasive doctrines of the Bible: that God is, quite literally, Almighty. Free will, the origin of evil, God's omniscience, creation, and the new birth are all presented within a Scriptural framework. The objections of those who do not believe in the Almighty God are considered and refuted. This edition also contains the text of the booklet, Predestination in the Old Testament.

Scripture Twisting in the Seminaries. Part 1: Feminism $5.95
John W. Robbins
   An analysis of the views of three graduates of Westminster Seminary on the role of women in the church.

The Trinity, Gordon H. Clark $8.95
   Apart from the doctrine of Scripture, no teaching of the Bible is more important than the doctrine of God. Clark's defense of the orthodox doctrine of the Trinity is a principal portion of a major new work of Systematic Theology now in progress. There are chapters on the deity of Christ, Augustine, the incomprehensibility of God, Bavinck and Van Til, and the Holy Spirit, among others.

What Do Presbyterians Believe? Gordon H. Clark $6.95
   This classic introduction to Christian doctrine has been republished. It is the best commentary on the Westminster Confession of Faith that has ever been written.

Commentaries on the New Testament

Colossians, Gordon H. Clark $6.95
Ephesians, Gordon H. Clark $8.95
First and Second Thessalonians, Gordon H. Clark $5.95
The Pastoral Epistles (I and II Timothy and Titus) $9.95
   Gordon H. Clark
   All of Clark's commentaries are expository, not technical, and

are written for the Christian layman. His purpose is to explain the text clearly and accurately so that the Word of God will be thoroughly known by every Christian. Revivals of Christianity come only through the spread of God's truth. The sound exposition of the Bible, through preaching and through commentaries on Scripture, is the only method of spreading that truth.

The Trinity Review

The Foundation's bimonthly newsletter, The Trinity Review, *has been published since 1979 and has carried more than sixty major essays by Gordon H. Clark, J. Gresham Machen, Fyodor Dostoyevsky, Charles Hodge, John Witherspoon, and others. Back issues are available for 40¢ each.*

Order Form

Name _____

Address _____

_____

Please: ☐ add my name to the mailing list for *The Trinity Review.* I understand that there is no charge for the *Review.*

☐ accept my tax deductible contribution of $ _____ for the work of the Foundation.

☐ send me _____ copies of *Colossians.* I enclose as payment $ _____ .

☐ send me the Trinity Library of 29 books. I enclose $135 as full payment for it.

☐ send me the following books. I enclose full payment in the amount of $ _____ for them.

_____

_____

_____

_____

_____

_____

_____

Mail to: The Trinity Foundation
Post Office Box 169
Jefferson, MD 21755

Please add $1.00 for postage on orders less than $10. Thank you.
For quantity discounts, please write to the Foundation.